Quite simply, there isn't much that Anne McNamara doesn't know about winning tenders. To get an insight into how she consistently delivers success - read this book- it could absolutely take your business to the next level.

Stuart Cairns
Partner. UK

BIRD & BIRD

Anne has written a masterpiece for anyone who to learn to win big new business has worked with Anne for years. She has single handedly overhauled our approach to pitching new business and tripled our win rate. This book will teach you how.

Bryce Maddock
CEO

TASKUS

Amanda Fisher
Managing Director Facilities Management, Defence and Justice

AMEY PLC

Anne is the definitive authority on bidding, together with her team she has created a unique business that cannot be matched on creativity or results when it comes to winning bids. Having worked with her over the last decade, she helped us secure multi-million-pound contracts, without her we would not have been able to maintain our market leading position.

Harry Townley
Business Development Director

BALFOUR BEATTY CONSTRUCTION 1994-2016

This is THE essential read for anyone wanting to learn how to win business and leave the competition in the cold. Anne transformed the way we bid for business and we closed a major deal immediately with the strategies; and the best part is, we had a blast doing it.

This book is packed with free resources, look for the following icons:

 Downloadable resource

 Free template

 elearning

1

CONTENTS

INTRODUCTION

> ## WHEN I GROW UP I WANT TO BE A WORLD CLASS BID MANAGER

...said nobody ever. But with a procurement market valued globally in the billions it is a serious industry with serious opportunities.

When I grew up I was either going to be a gaucho, riding around the plains looking moody, or an unelected benign dictator of Ireland. Surprisingly neither came off – but there's time yet.

In the meantime I found myself in the heart of capitalism selling high value products and services to enterprise and government. It was binary. You won or lost, with nothing in between. I liked it.

My win rate at the time was a respectable 50%, but what bothered me was that I didn't understand why we won or lost. I couldn't see a pattern of input to outcome. I decided that if I was to increase the odds of a win I had to develop a predictable winning methodology. So later when the one woman band grew into a team of intrepid adventurer-bidders we developed the ShineBid Winning Masterplan™

in Shine Bid. We've grown a business on the back of it and we now have a win rate between 78-82% every year. We work on hundreds of bids every year for our clients. We have won over $10bn in competition in 10 years and continue to optimise our process and increase our winning rates.

There is no mystery to winning at this level. It's part art, more science and involves a disciplined approach to winning. (Ah, discipline, isn't that the frustrating conclusion to being successful in all areas of life!)

That is why I wrote this book. It's a simple step by step methodology to generating predictable wins for your business, charity, department or agency.

ANNE MCNAMARA
ShineBid

IS THIS BOOK RIGHT FOR YOU?

If you are an organization that competes on differentiation, quality, innovation, and as well as price then read on. This book works at any value level or sector, it doesn't have to be a million-dollar contract, as long as there is a buyer and a bid you will see the benefit.

Winning Big has five parts to it:

1	2	3	4	5
THE BIDDING LANDSCAPE	THE WINNING MINDSET	GET FIT TO FIGHT	THE **SHINE**BID WINNING MASTERPLAN™	RESOURCES
		If you are not winning enough bids in your market or if you are entering a new market **start at Get Fit to Fight.**	If you are clear about your market and want to improve your win rate **start at the ShineBid Winning Masterplan™.**	

Wherever you start, you'll find something to help you get an advantage over your competition and increase your win rate.

THE CHALLENGE

The challenge is to recognize that bidding isn't an administrative burden but an engine for growth.

So many organizations fail to see this. Bidding is where the magic happens. No other business activity requires you to constantly iterate and adapt to keep delivering value to your customers. It is the enemy of complacency and entitlement. Bidding rewards bravery, ideas and invention. Once we recognized this ourselves (it took a while), it was the start of a long love affair, and for our people this was the beginning of a career to be proud of.

THE **BIDDING** LANDSCAPE

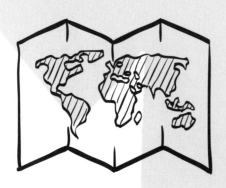

You are entering into rough terrain, but we will help you navigate through it, and enjoy the ride.

In this section, we'll give you the heads up on the key players - the Buyers, the Bidders and the language you need to know.

THE BUYERS

These are the main types of buyers involved in tendering, you will already be working with at least one of the categories. It should be obvious to you that these four groupings cover pretty much all organizations - bidding really is that pervasive.

GOVERNMENT

(Central government departments, state and local agencies- e.g. defense, commerce, children's services)

Procurement is non-negotiable. By law agencies must put tenders over a certain value out to competition.

Bidding to government and understanding their drivers requires additional insight - to learn more, download our eBooks detailed overleaf; How to Bid for Government Contracts in the USA and How to Bid for Government Contracts in the UK

LARGE ENTERPRISE/ COMMERCIAL

(Fortune 500's, listed or privately owned large to mid-cap companies)

Procurement is non-negotiable. Corporate governance rules ensure tenders over a certain value go out to competition.

NON-GOVERNMENTAL ORGANIZATION

(International aid agencies, arm's length government funded bodies, non-profits)

Procurement is non-negotiable. Governance rules require contracts over a certain value must be put out to competition.

OTHER COMMERCIAL ORGANIZATIONS

(Listed or privately owned small-cap companies)

Procurement is non-negotiable for listed companies and is common practice for the rest.

THE BIDDERS

In my experience there are four types of bidders. Which one are you?

PERFORMANCE BIDDERS

INDUSTRIAL BIDDERS

These are companies that generate 90%+ of their revenue from competitive bidding through a highly regulated process (e.g. defense contractors, specialist federal/government IT contractors, large infrastructure). Performance bidders have it nailed. They bid only for high value contracts where they have a high percentage chance of winning. They have a high volume of bids and a dedicated team of experienced bidders, driven to win. They are the early adopters of new ideas, methods and technologies and foster a culture of winning and innovating. They have tried and tested processes that team members adopt and buy into. As such they have a high win rate (above 70%).

These are companies that generate 75% of their revenue from competitive bidding through a highly regulated process. Unlike performance bidders they do not have it nailed. Whilst they may be focused on the right bid within their sector or specialism, they don't market test the chance of success and instead focus on 'getting the bid in'. They do not engender a culture of winning, it's a churn and volume game. The methodologies and processes they use are built around internal compliance rather than winning. As such they have a medium/low win rate (below 50%).

RELUCTANT BIDDERS

LIFESTYLE BIDDERS

These are companies for whom bidding is a requirement only some of the time. While they may be able to negotiate their way into an exclusive role occasionally, they cannot guarantee growth on this model. They resist bidding and view it solely as a response document. Likely to have little to no in-house experienced bidders. RFP's will be completed by a combination of sales/marketing/admin. Because the reluctant bidder is not strategic in their choice of bids they will often be relatively low in value and perceived to be a 'chore'. With resistance to bidding, no bidders and no track record of success the win rate is likely to be low (below 30%).

These are companies for whom bidding is a requirement only some of the time. Lifestyle bidders know what works for their business model. They are strategic in what they bid for and will have done their homework well in advance of the RFP going live. They will bid for less than 5 contracts a year and will measure at each stage of their bid their likelihood of winning. Likely that C-suite will be involved in managing the process, utilizing all resources at their disposal, bids will be creative, innovative and of high value and importance to the business. They are likely to have a high win rate (above 70%).

DOWNLOAD HOW TO WIN GOVT CONTRACTS USA
shinebidservices.com/resources

DOWNLOAD HOW TO WIN GOVT CONTRACTS UK
shinebidservices.com/resources

THE BID ROLES

We have worked with over 70 bidding companies and nearly 1,000 bids in over 20 verticals. While there is considerable commonality across them, each bidder approaches their team roles slightly differently. Large multi-territory organizations will have dedicated people in each role, and as you would expect smaller organizations will have one or two people performing all the roles and their functions.

Depending on your company size and which of the four types of bidders you identify with, use this section to build your bid team roles.

STRATEGIC PURSUITS LEAD/BUSINESS DEVELOPMENT LEAD

Purpose: The horizon scanner, on the hunt for new strategic clients, allowing the rest of the sales team to focus on conversion and growth of existing business and near side targets.

Bid Activities: Identify key targets and logos that will build the revenue and reputation of the company. Their job is to build up intelligence on the target and increase their profile with the companies that they are pursuing. They develop targeted marketing to get access to clients, including attending conferences, meet-ups, sponsoring sessions, becoming speakers at events where the targets are. They are also building up their intelligence.

You may find the job being done by: CEO, VP Sales, Head of Work Winning

Also known as: Whale Hunters

Rudely referred to as: The Face

Salary level: $$$$

HEAD OF WORK WINNING

Purpose: To generate sales from new and existing contacts and leads.

Bid Activities: Takes over from the Strategic Pursuits Lead. Balancing the resource investment in an RFP versus another warm deal is a constant juggle for them. They contribute to the bid strategy, feed information through to the researcher and bid director.

You may find the job being done by: CEO, Strategic Pursuits Lead, Manager of an existing contract that is coming up for renewal

Rudely referred to as: Heavy drinkers

Salary level: $$$$

CAPTURE MANAGER

Purpose: Influencing customer requirements as part of business development.

Bid Activities: Comes alive once you have decided to bid and before the bid comes to market. Develops a capture plan that defines the opportunity, assesses the environment, gets resources together and leads positioning of your offer with the customer. Ensures all internal stakeholders are aligned and on message.

You may find the job being done by: VP Sales, CEO

Rudely referred to as: Rarely subjected to rude names because not often seen on a bid

Salary level: $$

RESEARCHER/ANALYST

Purpose: To bring together the information available about the buyer and the tender opportunity. To turn information into intelligence so the bid team can develop the win strategy.

Bid Activities: Downloads target knowledge from the Strategic Pursuits Lead. Drives the research gathering on buyer's incumbents, competitors and markets. Defines the key areas to research. Does the research. Crafts this into analysis to contribute to the winning solution.

You may find the job being done by: Bid Manager, Bid Director, Bid Writer

Rudely referred to as: Nosey

Salary level: $$

ACCOUNT MANAGER/ RELATIONSHIP MANAGER

Purpose: Looks after the relationship with a current customer, identifies opportunities for selling deeper and wider, develops relationships with key people in customer organizations.

Bid Activities: Provides intelligence on the customer pain points, gets involved in solution development, provides feedback and steer to bid team.

You may find the job being done by: VP Sales, CEO

Rudely referred to as: Gatekeeper

Salary level: $$

BID DIRECTOR

Purpose: The owner of the bid. The main interface with the buyer.

Bid Activities: Involved deeply with the buyer. Works closely with the Strategic Pursuits Lead. Navigates your company's needs and the offer to the buyer to secure a win. Owns the governance process internally. Selects the bid team. Drives the intelligence. Develops the win strategy. Writes little, reviews all. Protects the strategy.

You may find the job being done by: VP Sales, Bid Manager, CEO

Rudely referred to as: Dictator

Salary level: $$$$

BID/PROPOSALS MANAGER

Purpose: The person responsible for bringing the bid together. They drive the process, coordinating the input from the bid team and the information from the Bid Director. They are responsible for the final production of the tender document.

Bid Activities: Works very closely with the Bid Director. They work with the Bid Director to select the team. Collates the intelligence. They issue the bid deliverables to the team, define the deadlines and the review processes. Coordinates between Subject Matter Experts, Bid Excellence Lead, and Bid Director. They will write and recraft much of the bid.

You may find the job being done by: VP Sales, Bid Manager, CEO, Proposals Manager

Rudely referred to as: The Understudy

Salary level: $$

COMMERCIAL MANAGER

Purpose: Price the bid to win.

Bid Activities: Develops pricing for tenders, leads commercial negotiations with buyers and supply. Finds savings and efficiencies to support win strategy. Manages contracts, resources and risks. Writes the commercial section.

You may find the job being done by: Bid Director, CEO

Rudely referred to as: Penny Pincher

Salary level: $$

BID /PROPOSALS CO-ORDINATOR

Purpose: To assist the Bid Manager.

Bid Activities: This role does whatever is required by the Bid Manager. This may involve writing, chasing copy, collating content, keeping notes on progress, assisting at writing workshops, reviewing, proofreading.

You may find the job being done by: Bid Manager, Writer, Office Assistant

Rudely referred to as: Dogsbody

Salary level: 💲

BID CONCEPT / BRAND DESIGNER

Purpose: To design the bid concept and branding for the bid.

Bid Activities: They use the intelligence and the win strategy to develop a compelling identity that represents what the bid offers.

You may find the job being done by: Graphic Designer

Rudely referred to as: Pre-Madonna

Salary level: 💲💲

BID GRAPHIC DESIGNER

Purpose: To design the bid to have maximum impact on the reader.

Bid Activities: Take copy and design it in line with the bid brand, develop visuals and infographics to enhance content.

You may find the job being done by: Bid Designer, Bid Manager

Rudely referred to as: Slow

Salary level: 💲💲

APP/DIGITAL DESIGNER

Purpose: To take the print version and digitize it.

Bid Activities: Using software and programming and working with Bid Director and Manager and Brand Designer.

You may find the job being done by: Graphic Designer

Rudely referred to as: The IT guy

Salary level: 💲💲

BID EXCELLENCE LEAD

Purpose: The guru of greatness. They identify excellence in bidding systems, strategy, and winning practices and drive it out across the organization.

Bid Activities: They keep up with international best practice. Review what's emerging across internal bid practice and lessons learned from previous bids. Capture it in writing. Explore bid technology. Disseminate, train and maintain standards.

You may find the job being done by: Bid Manager, Bid Researcher/Analyst, Bid Writer

Rudely referred to as: Annoying

Salary level: $$$

THE SUBJECT MATTER EXPERT (SME)

Purpose: To provide input on specialist subject matter. Ideally able to write it up but not always.

Bid Activities: Provides technical guidance on how the bidder meets the requirement of the procurer in a specialist area. It may be a technical solution or a detailed description of the company's process.

You may find the job being done by: Writer, Bid Manager, Bid Director, The Solution Generator, Google search

Rudely referred to as: Hard work

Salary level: $$$$

THE SOLUTION GENERATOR

Purpose: To bring their targeted expertise to work with the bid leadership to craft an innovative solution that delivers the win strategy, it could be financial, technical, a new value add, behavioral or procedural.

Bid Activities: To bring deep expertise in a specialist area that can generate an advantage for the bidder.

You may find the job being done by: SME, Bid Writer, Bid Manager, Bid Director

Rudely referred to as: Excitable

Salary level: $$

BID WRITER

Purpose: To write the responses to the bid questions.

Bid Activities: Write responses from scratch, or from a content depository, or from interviewing an SME. Improve the readability of all responses. Edit tone and consistency across the bid. Write the executive summary.

You may find the job being done by: Bid Manager, Subject Matter Expert, Bid Director

Rudely referred to as: Rarely subjected to rude names as seen as heroes

Salary level: $$

PROOF-READER

Purpose: Final edit and polish as the bid is ready for submission.

Bid Activities: Reviews and proofs all copy. Does not engage with the content other than readability and flow.

You may find the job being done by: Bid Director, Bid Manager, Writer, Subject Matter Expert

Rudely referred to as: Nit-picky

Salary level: $$

PRESENTATION/COLLABORATION COACH

Bid Activities: Presentation facilitation, coaching, collaborative behaviors coaching.

You may find the job being done by: Bid Director

Rudely referred to as: White Witch/Guru

Salary level: $$$$

THE LANGUAGE

This is a list of commonly used procurement terms in the US and Europe. It is not an exhaustive list, we've tried to cover the main terms, you will invariably collect more on your bidding journey.

Award Criteria
The criteria by which a contract is to be awarded.

Best And Final Offer (BAFO)
Following clarification / negotiation, the bidder's final offer not subject to further discussion.

Bid
Generic term for the document you submit to a buyer for work in a competition.

Bidder
The organization competing for the contract through a competition.

Buyer
The organization buying the goods, services or works.

Capability Statement
A one or two pager summarizing an organization's background, their core competencies, experience, capabilities, and past performance.

CAGE Code
The Commercial and Government Entity - is a five-character ID number that identifies government contractors. Used by the Department of Defense, the Department of Transportation and NASA, among other federal government agencies.

Central Contractor Registration (CCR)
A register operated by many federal, state, and local government agencies that requires a potential bidder to be registered with them before they do business with you.

Contracting Authority (CA)
The government/public-sector body buying goods, services or works.

Contracting Officer (CO)
The person(s) with the authority to enter into, administer, and/or terminate contracts.

Contracting Officer's Representative (COR)
COR will assist the Contracting Officer in administering specific aspects of a contract, will provide financial or technical expertise.

Contract Notice
An advertisement notifying suppliers of a contract opportunity.

D

Disabled Veteran-Owned Business Enterprise (DVBE)

A small business that is at least 51% owned and controlled by a service-disabled veteran of the military.

E

Evaluation Criteria

The method by which a tender response is marked.

Expression Of Interest (EOI)

A request to advise the procurer that you are interested in the tender opportunity.

F

Federal Acquisition Regulation (FAR)

A standardized set of regulations used by all federal agencies in making purchases.

Federal Acquisition Streamlining Act (FASA)

Law enacted in 1994 to simplify US government buying procedure, and lower barriers to procurement.

Federal Fiscal Year

The federal fiscal year runs from October 1 and to the following September 30.

Fair And Reasonable Price

A price that is fair to both parties and is subject to statutory and regulatory limitations.

Framework Agreement

A formal agreement with selected suppliers.

G

General Services Administration (GSA)

A centralized federal procurement and property management agency, GSA acquires products and communications for government offices and provides office solutions for federal employees.

GSA Schedule Contracts

Indefinite delivery, indefinite quantity (IDIQ), long-term contracts which involve pre-negotiated prices, delivery terms, warranties, and other terms and conditions which streamline the buying process.

I

Invitation For Bid (IFB)

This bid method is typically used as part of a sealed bid process. Contract is usually awarded to the lowest priced bidder.

Invitation To Participate In Dialogue (ITPD)

The document inviting bidders to participate in a competitive dialogue procedure.

Invitation To Tender (ITT)

The suite of tender documents issued to bidders invited to tender for a contract.

M

Minority Business Enterprises (MBE)
Minority businesses must be at least 51% minority-owned operated and controlled.

O

Official Journal Of The European Union (OJEU)
The official publication in which all high-value public sector contracts in the European Union must be advertised.

Open Procedure
Procurement method for high-value public sector contracts. Suppliers can apply without prior selection for example through a Pre-Qualification Questionnaire.

P

Past Performance Information Retrieval System (PPIRS)
The government wide single repository of contractor past performance data. The only authorized application to retrieve performance information.

Pitch
Generic term for the document you submit to a buyer for work in a competition.

Point Of Contact (POC)
A person or a department serving as the focal point of information concerning the procurement activity.

Pre-Bid Or Pre-Proposal Conferences
A meeting for bidders held by the buyer after the Invitation to Bid or Request for Proposal. Buyers will typically present the project, and bidders get the opportunity to understand more and ask questions.

Pre-Qualification Questionnaire (PQQ)
A questionnaire used to shortlist bidders and invite them to tender.

Pre-Solicitation Notice
Provides notice that a solicitation will be released and solicits capability responses from bidders.

Prime Contract
A contract awarded directly by the Federal government.

Procurement
The process of buying goods and services.

Proposal
Generic term for the document you submit to a buyer for work in competition.

R

Restricted Procedure
Procurement method for high-value public sector contracts. Supplier are selected by an open first-round invitation e.g. a Pre-qualification Questionnaire.

Request For Information (RFI)
Used to gather information to inform buying decision.

Request For Proposal (RFP)
A formal request for a proposal.

Responsible Procurement
Also known as sustainable procurement, generally considered to be a procurement process that takes into account social, environmental and economic impacts.

Request For Quote (RFQ)
When a buyer asks a firm to submit a quote for the specific activity or item.

 Solicitation Announcement
Used to inform potential suppliers of the goods or services to be procured.

Solicitation Document
Used to request potential suppliers submit a quotation, bid or proposal to provide the goods, services or works to be procured.

Small Business Specialist
Employed by the Federal government buying office to help small businesses with bidding to government. Most federal buying offices will have one.

Standard Selection Questionnaire (SSQ)
A questionnaire used to shortlist bidders and invite them to tender.

Statement Of Work (SOW)
A detailed statement that defines the buyer's entire scope of work and requirements.

Supplier Diversity
A proactive business program aimed at attracting small and diverse suppliers into the supply chain.

Tender
Generic term for the process of submitting an application to bid for work in a competition.

Woman Owned Businesses (WOB)
A small business that is at least 51% owned and controlled by a woman.

THE **WINNING** MINDSET

WHAT IT TAKES TO WIN

Winning is a mindset. As the leader of a company focused on nothing else but winning competitions it amazes me how much effort teams put into expressing dissatisfaction about the process, the expectations or the 'stupidity' of the buyers.

We only have so much energy, creativity and prefrontal cortex processing time available to us every day. Don't waste it on this negative nonsense. Decide you are going to love submitting a bid. Be as committed to this as you are to anything else that is important in your life, such as your health, your children or your relationship, and no this does not mean you should start chanting – "it's ours to lose". You need the bravery to challenge, the wisdom to know when not to and the tenacity to never give up. Don't whine. Get good and win stuff.

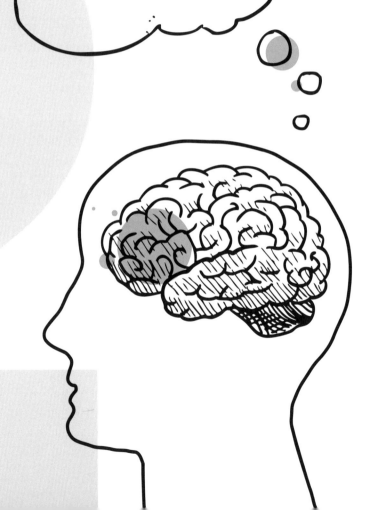

A winning mindset must be accompanied by winning behaviors. I frequently come across bid leaders who have the right mindset, but who are also egotistical lone-rangers who alienate customers and colleagues. Bidding is a people business that feeds on good relationships. But there is no denying it is a high-pressure environment to work in. It is why the industry attracts alpha men and women - people who thrive on competition, have mental toughness, bags of confidence and are calm under pressure. The flip-side of people with alpha characteristics is that they are a real liability in bidding. The need to dominate, to win at all costs, and cocky arrogance are traits that are incompatible with the collaborative working that it takes to win. Winning behaviors come naturally to people who show high levels of emotional intelligence (EQ) - these include the qualities of empathy, self-awareness, accountability, humility, self-control and maturity. These are the winning behaviors that we look for, they are fundamental to collaboration, and these are part of our new hire selection process.

+ Empathy
+ Active listening skills
+ Solution-focused
+ Commitment
+ Consistency
+ Supportiveness
+ Respect

The importance of collaborative working has also just dawned on buyers in a big way, particularly on long-term, complex contracts. Buyers are exhausted by adversarial relationships with suppliers, which add insult to injury by ultimately delivering mediocre outcomes. They want to work with people who are interested in mutual benefit, who have a can-do attitude, can handle criticism, offer constructive advice, and work with them as a team. I often hear buyers complain "If only we knew what they were really like to work with before we selected them". Buyers are doubling down on this, collaboration is increasingly becoming part of award criteria. Across Europe we are now seeing buyers asking bidders to take part in collaborative assessments during the bid period - these can be intensive workshops, one to one interviews or written tests or all of the above. The bid team will be observed by behavioral psychologists, judging every action. Are you ready for this level of scrutiny? My advice is to hire the best people who have high levels of EQ.

WHAT SORT OF BIDDER ARE YOU?

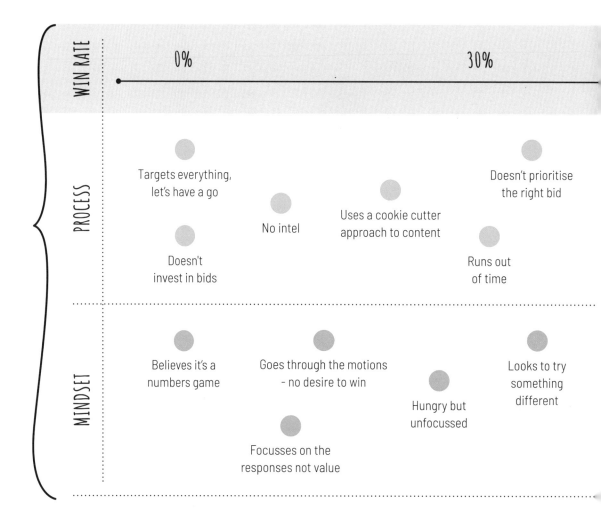

WIN RATE

0%   30%

PROCESS

Targets everything,
let's have a go

Doesn't prioritise
the right bid

No intel

Uses a cookie cutter
approach to content

Doesn't
invest in bids

Runs out
of time

MINDSET

Believes it's a
numbers game

Goes through the motions
- no desire to win

Looks to try
something
different

Hungry but
unfocussed

Focusses on the
responses not value

50% 70% 100%

Has tried and tested
systems & methodologies

Reviews performance &
learns from lost bids

Driven to achieve
return on investment

Does intel to
assess bid/no bid

Brings in experts and
3rd parties to enhance
learning & skills

Invests in researching the
client & the competition

Analyses research &
challenges assumptions

Innovative with
business buy-in

Committed

Focussed
on winning

Team players understand
you can't bid on your own

Strives to improve
teams & systems

Encourages
feedback

Thinks
outside the box

GET FIT TO FIGHT

We see so many companies using a scatter gun approach to contracts and how they present themselves. For one RFP they are targeted solutions experts, in another they are volume players.

One buyer is big government who wants strict compliance and governance processes but the next buyer is a start-up who wants agility. The cost of responding to these RFP's while reinventing yourself is often unviable. Assuming that they win the contract, the cost of setting up the service or product will be ridiculously high. If you are Google you have the breadth, depth and budget to do this, but for the rest of us it's not a wise growth strategy. You need to question and interrogate your company's purpose and direction.

The companies that fit into the category of Performance Bidder are by their nature focused on their targets and their fitness for purpose. They shape their market, lead the development of new product and service lines, and are highly integrated with the development needs of their clients. While the status quo remains stable, they stay fit. But even these giants of defense, aerospace, utilities and security get to the stage where major changes in the landscape force a re-evaluation and they need to pivot their approach. Lifestyle Bidders also fall into this category, focusing on fewer and farming more specific opportunities, and choosing

only to bid for the contracts that are an exact fit for their offer or purpose. The other two categories – Industrial and Reluctant - would be well advised to spend time in assessing their fitness.

Very few companies 'Get Fit to Fight' or 'Positioned' because of lack of knowledge, lack of time or in many cases lack of discipline. In truth, most dive into a bid opportunity, do their best and then see what happens. But if you find that you are reinventing yourself for every opportunity, your win rate is low and the cost of post-win mobilization is high, then read on.

BIDDING IS A ROUTE TO GROWTH. GET GOOD OR GET OUT. THERE ARE NO MEDALS FOR PARTICIPATION AND SADLY SECOND PLACE IS A LOSS. LOSING MEANS THAT YOU WILL HAVE A BIG FAT FIGURE ON THE WRONG SIDE OF THE P+L CALLED BID COSTS. IT'S AN EXPENSIVE BUSINESS THAT REQUIRES A LOT OF BRAINPOWER, INVESTMENT, TIME AND ENERGY. PARADOXICALLY, THERE ARE TWO WINNERS IN BIDDING. THE WINNER OF THE COMPETITION AND THE ONE WHO WALKED AWAY BECAUSE THEY HAD DONE THEIR PREPARATION AND KNEW NOT TO ENTER A FIGHT THEY WEREN'T READY TO WIN.

BATTLE

Getting ready to bid is like preparing for battle. You can't be fit to fight if you are vague on what you are fighting for and who you are fighting to get it. It took us years to work out that we were not ready for many of the opportunities we targeted. We took a step back and asked ourselves some basic questions. This was one of the main factors behind the increase in our win rates.

In 2011, a Fortune 250 company that we worked with won eight contracts in five months to provide an education service. The combined value was $300m. The margins and costs were in line with their other education activities. They were an experienced education provider, but this was a new service line, with different buyers and different expectations. While this was addressed on paper in their bids this was never fully appreciated in operational delivery. Over the course of the contract the company faced considerable challenges in delivering the contracts to the new format. In 2013, these eight contracts were all loss making and played a large part in wiping out 17% of the share value when the contracts concluded 24 months later.

So, what went wrong? These guys were good at education and great bidders. The problem was they weren't fit for this new contract type. It required a lot more pre-implementation consultation than they were used to in previous contracts. The company had a tried and tested mobilization and implementation process which did not apply in the new style contract. This new world required considerable investment upfront to review design solutions and pathways. The team were not equipped to deal with the level of consultation required early in the contract. The leaders were implementers and not consultants. A basic but crucial issue.

Just because it was education it didn't mean that they were best placed to capitalize on it. They not only lost millions and wiped out capital value, they also lost the opportunity cost of operating in a space where they were fit to win or they could have used that time to become agile in a different market.

How did they get back on track? We took them through our Get Fit to Fight Program over 10 days, which enabled them to refocus and prepare for their new world reality.

1

 2

3

 4

 5

WHERE YOU ARE NOW?

Define how you are doing now

Look at your performance over the last 18 months:

+ Achievements
+ Successes
+ Disappointments
+ Revenues
+ Targets met/not met

WHERE DO YOU WANT TO BE?

What does your market place look like?

Define where you currently fit in the market

WHAT DOES THE MARKET NEED?

Define the market need

Segment clients by their needs, maturity, size, industry, behaviors or persona

WHAT IS STOPPING YOU?

What or who are the barriers and blockers to growth?

What has been done to date to overcome them?

Create a joined-up Business Development strategy

BRING IT ALL TOGETHER IN A CLEAR VALUE PROPOSITION

Create an authentic value proposition

Focus the proposition on the right targets

FINDING THE RIGHT OPPORTUNITIES

The sweet spot in bidding is to get involved in an impending contract opportunity just before it has been rubber stamped by the buyer's own approval process. At this point, you know it's real and not going to be mothballed, and the requirements are not set in stone. This is an opportunity to seriously influence the buyer – your aim is to get close to them during this 'pre-bid phase' and get them to define requirements only you can deliver. Failing this, at the least you will have done positive messaging about yourself and picked up valuable intelligence. You only really get this chance to engage the buyer if you have an existing relationship or you've been trying to create one.

Buyers rarely enter big deals with companies they have not heard of or not carried out soft market testing with. The message here is to be proactive, meet regularly with your targets about their plans and their pain points. If you don't have a relationship, get on their radar by moving into their environment. If you are a contractor who is a specialist in healthcare, you need to be seen as a credible contributor to health care by producing or sponsoring valuable insights, learning or knowledge. If you are a SaaS player for example targeting charities, add value to the charity sector by sponsoring charity events that buyers engage with.

If you are pursuing a government contract, you can find out about them easily because they are advertised publicly. There are hundreds of portals you can use to find out about these opportunities. Some are free. You set up an account and create a profile and then are alerted every time you match an opportunity, a bit like a dating site. Most public bodies operate an open door for suppliers to discuss upcoming opportunities so don't be afraid of making contact with them, you will not prejudice your chances.

TARGET BIDS

BID OPPORTUNITIE

BID/NO BID

Bid more win more. This is the faulty thinking of bidders when under pressure to deliver results. "We have a 50% win rate, let's get growth by bidding more". This is chasing revenue and not margin. You need to focus on improving your productivity and efficiency, not volume. How do you do this? First, recognize this is what you are doing. Second, make sure you're fit to fight, this will help you become more selective about which bids to go for. Third, adopt the ShineBid Winning Masterplan™ and you will see a tangible increase in your win rate.

DOWNLOAD THE MASTERPLAN
shinebidservices.com/resources

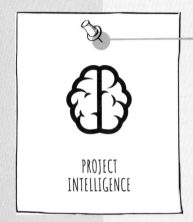

PROJECT INTELLIGENCE

CREATING A WIN STRATEGY

THE **SHINE**BID

WINNING MASTERPLAN™

Now you're ready to bid, use the ShineBid Winning Masterplan™ to develop winning bids. It is a simple effective 10 step process, focusing on the crucial activities that make the winning difference in bidding.

The ShineBid Winning Masterplan™ is a culmination of our learning over the last decade. It has been developed through an iterative process of creating, doing, failing, starting again, refining, testing, championing, and reviewing. The full masterplan is in the resources section in the back of the book.

SOLUTION DEVELOPMENT

BRANDING YOUR BID

SET UP AND MANAGEMENT

BUYER ENGAGEMENT

INTERVIEWS AND PRESENTATIONS

EXECUTIVE SUMMARY

PRODUCTION

WRITING AND REVIEW

PROJECT INTELLIGENCE

At ShineBid, we do not undertake any bid without intelligence. In my experience it is the most valuable, non-negotiable part of bidding. You cannot create a win strategy without intelligence on a) the buyer, what they are buying and what is important to them – or their 'buyer issues' and b) how you stack up against the competition.

When we first meet new clients, they reassure us that "we have all of the intel we need". This claim starts to unravel as soon as we start asking what they have and where they got it from. Solid intel turns out to be an unsubstantiated rumor or is so full of holes and speculation that no responsible person should let it anywhere near a bid. In this case no intel is better than bad intel.

One client, before they came to us, were given the wrong steer by a mid-ranking official within the buying organization that resulted in them bidding for four lots they wanted and two lots they didn't want, and the latter were at a ridiculously low price. The thinking was that if we go cheap on the ones we don't want we'll rule ourselves out. Unsurprisingly, they won the two lots they didn't want. This was entirely avoidable if they had verified their intel and used their own judgement.

Another issue we see in re-bids – bids where our client is the incumbent – is confirmation bias. Clients will have insider information but lack the objectivity or perspective to interpret it. This is not because they are incapable it's simply a human tendency to hear what you want to hear.

The single biggest piece of advice I can offer on doing bid intel is to start it before the bid becomes a bid. Before the constraints of a legal procurement process closes down any chance of an open conversation with the buyer. This is where you need to leverage the interplay between your sales and bidding activities to get in front of the buyer at the earliest opportunity.

INTEL ON THE BUYER

The deeper you understand the buyer, the better your chances of putting together a bid that exceeds their requirements and delivers a winning result. To do this, you need to understand and prioritize what's important to the buyer or what we call the 'buyer issues' – this is what you build your win strategy on – being better than the competition at hitting the buyer issues. For example, this could be cost certainty, security, management team, or business continuity. You develop your buyer issues by finding out about their pain points – their worries, challenges, blockers or risks. What problem is this contract going to fix? What's the backstory?

Here's a great example of how finding out the back story can change the fate of a bidder. Our client, an intellectual property advisory service, had been retained by a major international food company for the last 28 years. Out of nowhere, their contract was going out to competition. Why? There had to be a story behind it. We did our intel and found out the new owners of the food company were concerned that a 28-year-old relationship with one city firm may not be value for money. To turn things around, the food company replaced the longstanding internal contract manager and brought in a replacement. This individual was under pressure to deliver an immediate impact and the first action she did was to retender the contract.

Our first action was to get our client to move from their current position of responding to a bid document to a position where they actually engaged with the buyer's pain points. Could an incumbent really offer value for money? Would a new firm bring energy, innovation, new approaches and better value? It's not easy to win a rebid. If you come up with great ideas in the submission, the buyer's first question is why did you not do it before? We had to focus on the depth of understanding that the company had developed of the buyer over their 28-year relationship and the benefits of that continuity and the security that came with this. We helped our client capitalize on their knowledge of the buyer's strategic priorities and operational needs to develop solutions which gave them a superior position over the competitors and won them the bid.

INTEL ON THE COMPETITION

DOWNLOAD OUR COMPARATIVE ANALYSIS TOOL
shinebidservices.com/resources

How can you outdo your competitors if you don't know what they are going to offer? Most bidders will do a SWOT (Strengths, Weaknesses, Opportunities and Threats) analysis on their competitors at pre-bid stage. We are not keen on SWOT, it has many limitations, the biggest is that you can't prioritize the most important factors. Doing a comparative analysis between you and your competitors in each of the areas on the buyer issues is a more useful way of evaluating how you stack up against them. We've developed a simple comparative analysis tool which helps you to score and rank your position against the other bidders. It will give you a feel for which competitors you need to beat and where you should focus your energies. I would recommend doing the analysis with up to four of your serious competitors to not overcomplicate the task. You should rerun the analysis at regular checkpoints and every time you get hold of new intel on the opposition.

Once you're in the bid competition, you need to do a detailed competitor profile for each. Your aim is to understand their offer. What relationships do they have with the buyer? What will they do to win this job? Look at their market position, capabilities, competencies, bid team, business health, recent wins, losses and acquisitions. Scan their press coverage and company publications. Are they aggressive on cost? Do they go over the top on innovation? Which technologies do they tend to use? Which suppliers have they aligned with? You need a hyper-awareness of your competitors' moves. Then take the competitor profiles, pick the best attributes of all the competitors in the areas most important to the buyer and create the most formidable adversary you could possibly imagine - and you pit yourself against that.

There's a high probability one of your competitors will have the inside track with the buyer - either as the incumbent or some other shared history. You can do something about this if you find out early enough but you might just have to accept that you just won't have the buyer's ear on this one. On one bid for a housing development, we found out that the competition had been building a relationship with the customer for over a year, attending key meetings, investing in the area and getting close to the key decision-makers, showcasing what they had to offer.

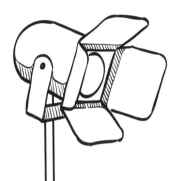

FOCUSING YOUR INTEL

" I WANT TO KNOW EVERYTHING ABOUT THE BUYER

Hold on! This way lies trouble. Yes, we advocate a thorough approach to research but this is just madness. Not everything about the buyer is important, don't waste time and effort on 'nice to knows', focus on the 'need to knows'. Consolidate what you already know, identify areas or where your intel is weak and then put a plan together to prioritize filling in these gaps.

GETTING YOUR INFORMATION

The first step of developing intel is information gathering. Around 80% of the intel you will need is out there in the public domain, so there's no need to stretch ethical boundaries. Of this, around 25% is online so don't just rely on secondary sources do some 'human collection' too – make some calls and speak to people, you'll be surprised what you can find out.

Top sources:

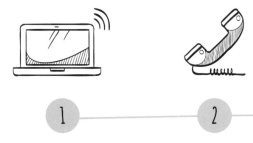

Google of course
– for context, background, big picture, visions, strategies, and biogs.

Customers themselves – every meeting, phone call and open day is a chance to get intel.

3

4

5

6

7

Colleagues – it's likely someone in your organization has worked for the competition or buyer.

Your network – your mates, ex-colleagues, get on to your LinkedIn connections.

Suppliers – they will have a good overview of your marketplace, having supplied many of your competitors.

Conferences/trade shows – it's a free for all, a vital source on your competitors (P.S. you don't need to wear your badge).

Industry experts/ consultants – it's a revolving door, experts like to talk about how much they know, and consultants are always on the lookout for the next commission.

SPEAKING TO EXPERTS

Getting information from people without letting on the purpose is a valuable intel gathering skill. If it's a warm or cold contact asking outright for information might make them feel like they are being interrogated. You can get people to voluntarily tell you things without asking through some useful conversational techniques. Why would people talk to you? Because it's human nature. We like to talk about ourselves, show off what we know, feel a bit superior. Here are three rudimentary conversational techniques to try, there's no tradecraft involved, you just need to do some homework in advance to know the right questions to ask.

Be humble – if you come across as humble or ignorant of a topic, knowledgeable people will feel compelled to educate you. For example, I wanted to find out more about the decision-making process on a future bid, I called the buyer's organization and opened with "I'm new to this sector" and "I really don't know how things work here". I sounded like I could really do with a helping hand. The person I spoke to went on to explain the organization structure, governance process and how decisions are made. A few well-timed follow-up questions gave me exactly what I was looking for. Play down your understanding, it's disarming, bow to their superior knowledge and they will provide information.

Be provocative – try lobbing a grenade, make an erroneous statement, something that will prompt the person to want to clarify, explain, defend against and in the process, reveal true information. For example, I wanted to validate whether an organization was increasing its capital investment program next year, during the conversation with them I calmly threw in "I had no idea you were doubling your capital investment program next year" – the response I got back "no that's not correct, we are increasing investment, but only by £10m or so" and then... "where did you hear that?" Be prepared to be probed about the source of your dodgy statement. Remember you are trying to provoke a reaction, you are not trying to offend them, so don't say anything too galling or silly.

Be silent – if you create an awkward silence in your conversation, it encourages the other person to keep talking just to fill in the gap. One time, I called an organization to find out more about an incumbent provider. I asked "do you have an incumbent provider" – "yes" was the reply, and then pause - long pause - it was awkward, the target felt uncomfortable so she started telling me about the incumbent just to fill the silence. This technique works very well on the phone. Don't rush in to talk, listen, be silent, let the other person do the talking.

FILTERING THROUGH YOUR INFORMATION

You have to sift through all the information you have gathered to find the most useful gems. Your first pass check is "Can I afford to ignore it?" If you can't, then ask yourself "So F****ing What?" to work out if the information is useful or peripheral. What does this mean? How will this influence the bid? This reflective process will probably help you to identify other illuminating avenues to pursue. Finally, how reliable is the information? Not all information is credible, an official press release is more trustworthy than an anonymous forum post. You have to rate the credibility of your sources, from low to high. Anything below high should be verified by at least two sources.

TURNING INFORMATION INTO INTELLIGENCE

You now have your filtered information, it has gone through the "So F****ing What?" wringer, met the "cannot ignore" criteria and rated high on the credibility test. To turn it into actionable intelligence, you need to extract some conclusions from it that will get you to the point where you can put together a prioritized list of buyer issues at the win strategy workshop – which is explained in the following chapter.

Many bidders make the mistake of dropping their intel gathering once they have the bones of their win strategy. As you move through the bid stages, new info will come to light. If you're not in front of this, you'll be operating in ignorance. Keep on gathering intel, when new intel comes in check your buyer issues against it or rerun the competitor comparative analysis tool again. You might need to refine, tweak or even bin your strategy.

Do not undertake any bid without intelligence, just don't do it.

Start your intel before the bid becomes a bid, and before the formal procurement process shuts down your access to the buyer.

Your intel needs to find out what's important to the buyer or what we call the 'buyer issues' – this is what you build your win strategy on.

Do a comparative analysis between you and your competitors to work out how you stack up against them.

CREATING A
WIN STRATEGY

A win strategy is the value proposition that you have come up with targeted directly at how you overcome the buyer issues. This is something that you commit to massively. You do not flirt with a win strategy. You wear it everywhere. It is an absolute commitment. The win strategy is your answer to "Why Us?". It is made up of your big sell and win themes.

DEVELOPING YOUR WIN STRATEGY

CREATE IT

The most effective way of developing a win strategy is to workshop it as a group. You cannot just meet around somebody's desk. Allocate at least two hours if you are in different locations and are video-conferencing in. If you have the luxury of all being together, calendar a four-hour session, with a facilitator.

First, you need to define and agree the buyer issues – this really starts to sing when you do this as a bid team, and this is where the team really starts to gel. Review the intel reports, we believe in documenting intel and producing thorough reports. Then analyze the buyer's requirements. Asking good quality questions here is where we really start to bring the analysis out, and this is what drives the win strategy. What point are they trying to get at? What are they really looking for? Why are they doing that? Through careful deliberation involving constructive challenge and debate, you will reach broad consensus on what the buyer issues are. You should have between three and five buyer issues – the absolutely most important things they care about.

Then comes the exciting bit - what do we do about it? You will generate many ideas and solutions that hit the buyer issues.

But you are looking for the one overarching big sell that answers the only important question there is 'Why Us?' The other, smaller nuggets are your supporting win themes, such as fast mobilization or competitive price. They tell the story of your bid and help you stand out from the competition. Most people think that the win themes are the big sell. They are definitely attention grabbers, but only the big sell will close the deal. At best, you do not want more than seven or eight win themes, and capture these in a win themes matrix, which we have handily supplied.

Example of win strategy development for a defense project

INTEL	BUYER ISSUES	WIN STRATEGY	
		BIG SELL	**WIN THEMES**
Buyer seeking fastidious approach, highly governed, and hugely compliant in running their operations If you do not massively respect their need for compliance then you are just adding to the pain point of this buyer	Compliance Operational continuity Risk management	Focused completely on compliance – 'Power on the ground' bringing power, rigor and a huge level of respect for process and compliance	Delivering 100% right first time Zero impact on existing operations **Note:** We actually created 32 processes and procedures that proved we could ensure 100% compliance

Example of win strategy development for an online hotel booking platform

INTEL	BUYER ISSUES	WIN STRATEGY	
		BIG SELL	WIN THEMES
The intel revealed how badly the platform was performing and the terrible customer ratings and feedback they were collating as a result	Improving their volume handling issues Improving customer experience	We do Happy! Our reason for being in business is to make your customers happy	What Good Customer services look like: first call resolution, speed of response times, multiple platform skills, 24/7 service, informed and well-trained personnel. Customer satisfaction KPIs
They were miles behind the competition and the issues all stemmed from terrible customer service			Good customer service as a resolution to their perceived volume issues. We evidenced our claims with statistics and data from other transformational cases with previous clients that had been in a similar situation
The client was in denial about their reality. They thought their issue was their inability to handle the volume not their inability to make their customers happy			

WIN THEME MATRIX

		Question					
		1 **Team**	**2** **Planning**	**3** **Programme**	**4** **Logistics**	**5** **Supply Chain**	**6** **Etc**
Big Sell and Win Themes	Leader in innovation	✓	✓	✓	✓	✓	✓
	Best in class collaborative working	✓	✓	✓		✓	
	National player with a local team	✓	✓			✓	
	Apprenticeship scheme for local young people	✓			✓	✓	
	Etc.						
	Evaluation weighting %						

COMMUNICATE IT

Once you have your win strategy, everyone in your team must live and breathe it. It must be at the front and center of their minds, so that when they are developing solutions, meeting buyers or writing responses they are consistently pushing this strategy through. Don't let a communication fail upend your strategy.

TEST IT

You have to test the strategy with the buyer. There should be touchpoints throughout the bid process, where you get to meet with the buyer to develop the solutions. You want to get a feel for what the buyer thinks by seeing how they react. If they are lukewarm, you may need to refine your strategy. If it's still not working, then you need to get back to base and check if your intel is right or if your buyer issues are off. Don't be afraid of iterating until you get the reaction you want – delight!

REVIEW IT

Review the win strategy at every major bid milestone. Sometimes, a key decision-maker will leave or a major event happens in your industry that could impact on your strategy, and you need to be able to react.

COMMIT TO IT

You spent so much energy and effort on creating the strategy, don't forget about it. You need to keep banging on that drum. It's the thread that runs through your bid. Too often you can lose sight of the strategy as you migrate through the bid.

SELL IT

In the bid responses, in the branding, in your interactions with the buyer, at the interviews, and presentations – sell it!

Create it - hold a win strategy session with the bid team to define buyer issues, big sell and win themes.

Communicate it - make sure all the team knows the bid strategy.

Test it - with the buyer to make sure it aligns to their requirements and expectations.

Review it - keep checking you're still on the right track.

Commit to it - don't lose the strategy along the way. Too often you can lose sight of the strategy as you migrate through the bid.

Sell it!

SOLUTION DEVELOPMENT

The win strategy drives all solution development. Your bid will comprise some big strategic solutions, for example the choice of technology for the contract or the location of the operations base, and many smaller solutions such as the sequence of mobilization activities or your approach to stakeholder engagement. Solutions must align to the win strategy – for example if your win strategy is about compliance and low risk for a defense project then you shouldn't propose a new to market un-tested solution. Carry out an analysis of the contract requirements to make sure you understand what the buyer is asking for. In government/public-sector bidding it can be quite straightforward to see from the evaluation criteria what's important to them. Sometimes you can really tell where the buyer's mind is because they ask the same question a number of times in different ways. Remember, the contract requirements don't always tell the full story. You need to understand their unstated requirements too - this is where your intel on the buyer issues comes into play by giving you broader context.

In my experience, the best solutions come from the pain points of the buyer. You must have the absolute confidence to explore their issues and then go back to your product/service lines and see how they can rise to the challenge. Most people do not bother doing this. They go to their service lines and ask "What do we have that we can sell them?" or think "We are great at this so let's tell them all about it". This is going to keep you at a 30% win rate. If you want to get above this, you need to step in to the buyer's shoes.

Some buyers know exactly the solution they are after – here your job is to talk them through how you'll deliver. Other buyers don't have a clue, and your role is to help them understand the problem and its solution. The Buyer Engagement chapter covers how to deal with this scenario in more detail. You cannot expect the buyer to know why your solution is better than the competitor. To overcome this, each solution should come with its own story. Use supporting analysis to show how you arrived at your proposed solution – for example the initial issue identified, the options you ruled out and why, and the benefits of this offer to the buyer. You can kill the credibility of a rival bidder if they propose a solution that you have already dismissed.

ITS A FIVE-STEP PROCESS

We use this five-step solution development process with our clients to help them develop the best solution for their bid.

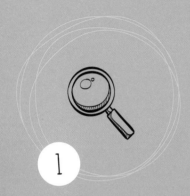

1

INVENT

Hold a structured workshop to brainstorm ideas with the bid team

Get subject matter experts involved – ensure they are focused on the buyer

Generate solutions. Consider:

+ New solutions
+ Adapting existing solutions

IDENTIFY

Interrogate the formal requirements. Consider:

What are they really asking for?

What is the problem that needs fixing?

How does this relate to our intel on the buyer issues?

ALIGN

3

Does it align with
the win strategy?

Capture any assumptions
so you can test
these with the buyer

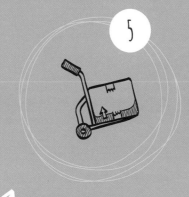

5

PACKAGE

Package up the
solution and present it

Be clear on the differences
between features (attributes of
your solution) and benefits (what
it means for the buyer)

Show supporting analysis - the
story of how you got to the
solution – use this to mitigate
competitor solutions

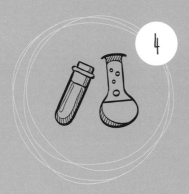

4

TEST

Test and review your issues, products,
and solutions with the buyer

Clarify with the buyer any
assumptions you've made

INNOVATION

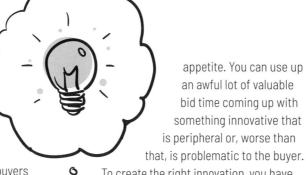

Innovation is a powerful differentiation strategy in bidding. It could be a big or small innovation in pricing, technology or process. You have to target innovation very clearly. Many buyers will use the word "innovation" because somebody has told them that they need to be more innovative. You will see it all over their tender documentation, and you will say "we have some great innovation we can give these guys". But, innovation in some organizations would not even warrant a mention in others. It is your job to unpack what they mean by innovation and their risk appetite. You can use up an awful lot of valuable bid time coming up with something innovative that is peripheral or, worse than that, is problematic to the buyer. To create the right innovation, you have to focus on the problem that needs to be solved. Do not get distracted with what your potential product offerings are.

If your win strategy is good value, cheap price, then your innovations are about cost reduction while maintaining service levels. If your win strategy is about speed of execution, fast mobilization, then your innovation efforts need to be in technologies, processes, and methodologies that support this. What we have found is most innovations that resonate with the buyer have been very simple process-driven, invented for the bid – innovations where we adapt our offer to the buyer requirement. It is as simple as that. For example, on a metro rail project, the buyer's new project approvals process was so complex that we reorganized it for them. Our bid showed them an optimized process that met all their regulatory requirements, cut down the time spent by 40% and importantly saved them money. Although it wasn't an exciting innovation for us, it was significant to the buyer.

The win strategy drives all solution development – the solution must align to the strategy.

Carry out an analysis of the requirements to make sure you understand what the buyer is asking for.

Tap into your intel on buyer issues to understand their unstated requirements.

Provide solutions the buyer wants, and not solutions based on what you have and can sell them.

Follow our five-stage process 'identify – invent – align – test – package' to develop your solutions.

BRANDING
YOUR BID

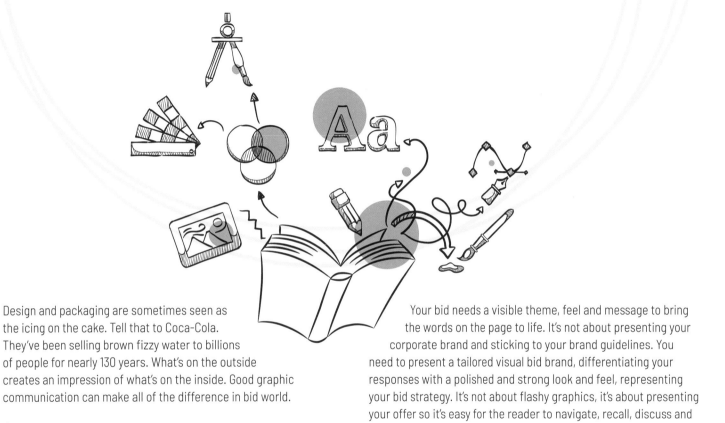

Design and packaging are sometimes seen as the icing on the cake. Tell that to Coca-Cola. They've been selling brown fizzy water to billions of people for nearly 130 years. What's on the outside creates an impression of what's on the inside. Good graphic communication can make all of the difference in bid world.

Your bid needs a visible theme, feel and message to bring the words on the page to life. It's not about presenting your corporate brand and sticking to your brand guidelines. You need to present a tailored visual bid brand, differentiating your responses with a polished and strong look and feel, representing your bid strategy. It's not about flashy graphics, it's about presenting your offer so it's easy for the reader to navigate, recall, discuss and explain – especially if you have dense technical submissions.

HOW TO DEVELOP A CONCEPT

A bid brand will create a whole set of associations rooted in your win strategy, making your bid stand out in every way. Don't design too early, or you end up spending time-consuming concepts based on an undefined story. You get your story from the intel and win strategy. Hold a briefing session for your designers with the bid team – get them to summarize the project context, key requirements, and most importantly your big sell and win themes. Your design team need to turn the big sell story into a more creative set of brand messages and visual designs, ones that make a buyer engage with the story. Here are examples of design concepts based on an undefined and defined story.

EXAMPLE 1

Big Builder is bidding for a £50m a year construction framework contract for a council in London. They have been the incumbent supplier for the last four years, and their contract is now up for renewal. Our client is shortlisted alongside six other companies of similar ability.

UNDEFINED STORY + NO WIN STRATEGY

If the big sell story isn't well defined, by default your option is to go generic focusing on the Council or Big Builder. This approach isn't targeted and is a missed opportunity for some clever messaging. This approach doesn't demonstrate that they understand the needs of the Council on this particular contract. It doesn't show that they have considered the competition and that they are thinking about what pain the Council are in and how to solve it. Here's how the undefined story plays out:

Design Concept 1: Big Builder has recently invested heavily in Research & Development (R&D) so our design is futuristic, has a running theme about research and why they are the most modern and innovative construction partner. Our design will use hi-tech styling with geometric patterns to give a feeling of them being a cutting-edge company.

Design Concept 2: Big Builder is one of the most experienced in London, so we are having a London-focused theme. The Union Jack is used, along with major landmarks and a tube map icon system throughout. We want them to know about our long history in the city so at the start of every section we will have a photograph of one of our London projects with some key achievement statistics.

DEFINED STORY + WIN STRATEGY

Now, we have our big sell, which is based on our intel and understanding of the buyer wants.
We know what's important to them, we know what makes their decision-makers tick.

Design Concept 3: Building Momentum - Big Builder have been the incumbent framework supplier for four years. We know the Council like Big Builder but are also looking for new ideas and approaches. They have recently started to appoint other competitors for similar works. We need to show that we have fresh energy, fresh ideas and that we are treating this contract renewal like they are a brand-new client, except with all the advantages that come with familiarity. This design concept will have punchy language and big messages. We will use bold typography for impactful headings and to convey that Big Builder is a partner that will continue to challenge the status quo at every turn. Our executive summary will also be structured page by page as an on-going journey. Each page completes a piece of a jigsaw that starts from 'where we were', to 'where we are' and 'where we are going'. No other contractor can do this. The early section of the executive summary will set the scene on how challenging things were before we arrived. 'Where we are' will show all of our big-ticket statistics that show where we have hit their targets or exceeded expectations, and the latter pages for 'where we are going' highlight our ambitious goals and what the benefits are to the Council.

Design Concept 4: Inside Track – As the incumbent, Big Builder are also in a unique position where for the next few months they can make additional impact during delivery, they have mature relationships in place to hit the ground running and they know the Council so well that they are more or less an extension of their team. This concept is about reminding the Council that choosing Big Builder means the lessons that have been learned together lead to better performance, cost savings and more innovation from the start. These are lessons about their culture or how they operate that won't need learning again. Lessons that a new contractor will have to learn from scratch. This design focuses on collaboration, insight and speed. We can use rich photography that shows Big Builder people with their people and in their community. Warm colors and softer typography will be used to focus less on bold and disruptive change, and more on continuing our collaborative journey of progression.

PRINT AND PACKAGING

If the bid requires print in final production, then consider the packaging and document format early during the concept design stage. This is also the case if the submission is digital and needs unique parameters set up or interactive features incorporated. Without a doubt one of the greatest challenges in the design process is the limited time there is to produce the design. However, this doesn't have to mean you are limited in how creative, bespoke, professional and premium bid documents can be.

Develop a tailored visual bid brand, differentiating your responses from your competitors.

Create your bid brand once you've developed the win strategy to avoid a generic design.

If you have a defined story, you can use your bid branding to convey key messages.

SET UP AND MANAGEMENT

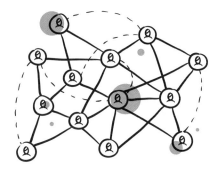

When I first got into this business over a decade ago this was the prevailing approach:

+ The bidder would find out about a bid or re-bid when it was a widely known fact.

+ Their sales guy would maybe have a meeting or two with the buyer, on his own. Notes may or may not be taken.

+ An internal meeting might be held to get ready for the bid but no real action took place until the 'real' bid came out.

+ Once out, a proposal manager would be thrown in, who would hastily allocate questions to different authors.

+ The commercial and legal people would dive in and start assessing contract risk and cost.

+ The writers would work independently on their allocated questions with limited context and direction.

+ The commercials and legal people would inevitably drive their bid approach based on their attitude to risk and pricing.

+ The proposal manager would bring the document together, navigating the commercial and legal bias and the solutions in the responses.

The end result was about a 50% win rate. In retrospect, this was down to the inability of the competition to do any better. It's only when we introduced a disciplined approach to how we worked that we saw a significant upturn in our win rates. Crucial to this, is setting up the bid correctly from the start. If you don't set up right, you risk being overwhelmed by the issues that will be thrown at you. It will be hard to catch your breath or make changes midway.

GETTING THE BEST TEAM

We've worked with clients who don't put their best people on their bid, they think the strength of their brand is enough to get them through. This false belief has seen egg on the face of many big hitters who miss out on contracts they thought they were a shoe in for. We've also worked on bids, usually high-profile ones, where the client's people are all over it – it's like having five different Michelin star chefs working in your kitchen. There can only be one bid boss – the person with overall responsibility for the bid, who can make unilateral decisions, who will sign off the win strategy and will direct and motivate the bid team. The bid boss is supported by a team representing the different scope areas of the contract, for example, operations, HR, finance, legal. The expertise might be in-house already, or you might need to bring in consultants, or partner up with another organization. On page 12, we describe the key roles in a bid team – you might not need all of them, but you should make it your mission to make sure each one is filled by the best person for the job, and not just whoever's at a loose end. If you cannot put names next to the roles, or you have the same name in every box, you have a problem and you should read the Get Fit to Fight chapter to understand what you are trying to achieve through bidding.

THE CONTROL SHEET

When you receive the documentation for a tough government tender, it will be about an inch thick. A third of the document will cover general information, a third covers the bid deliverables (the questions you need to answer), and the final third are the appendices (for example the contract). Most people take the bid deliverables, drop them into Excel, allocate responsibilities to no-name people i.e. "Security" or "HR".

We on the other hand, get the bid deliverables, and create a 'control sheet'. The control sheet captures everything you need to know about the bid - the requirements, content needs, ownership, scores & weightings, deadlines and format/page restrictions. The control sheet is our proven tool for managing the production of bids - it has worked with different bids and different buyers. We developed it in Word, it contains key columns, and headings. To populate it, you have to resolve some important issues, for example, the timing of solution development; when experts need to input into the process; who is writing each response; what support they need; when and who is doing the peer reviews and sign-offs. The control sheet will go through many iterations.

The control sheet in a complex bid will take approximately two hours to three-quarters of a day to complete. We recommend that the bid boss undertakes this seemingly basic admin task. Do not give it to a random assistant. This has nothing to do with skill - it is about getting buy-in to the requirements of the buyer. This is probably the most productive time the bid boss can spend at the outset of the process.

On the next page, we have included our control sheet template for free, you don't need to reinvent the wheel or complicate your life. We haven't seen anything in bidding that the control sheet couldn't handle.

CONTROL SHEET TEMPLATE

Headlines

PROJECT	[Enter project name here]
BID BOSS	[Name][Email][Phone][Mobile]
KEY BID CONTACTS	
KEY DEADLINES	[Key Deadline][Date]

Key Dates and Bid Production Timetable

ACTIVITY	DEADLINE
Agree bid strategy and bid production actions	[Date]
Answer planning for questions and templates completed	[Date]
Develop bid brand	[Date]
Issue question response templates	[Date]
Drafts produced by authors/contributors	[Date]
Sign off on bid brand	[Date]
Authors issue first drafts of responses and appendices	[Date]
Review of drafts	[Date]
Update of response drafts and appendices	[Date]
Clarifications deadline	[Date]
Sign off of designed bid	[Date]
Print deadline	[Date]
Upload of submission	[Date]

Notes and submission requirements: [Insert any notes about the submission eg. Font size, file formats, page/word limits]

Detailed Control Sheet Content for Questions

[SECTION NAME]								
Ref	Question	Weighting (If applicable)	Response Headlines	Responsible	Contributors	Page Limits (or word count)	Draft Deadline	Final Deadline
[XX]	A schedule and details of the proposed materials, finishes and components to new and retained areas	15%	Materials Outline	Rod	Jane	1	2pm 6/8	9am 14/8
			Materials Palette Interiors	Jane	Rod	1	2pm 7/8	9am 15/8
			Materials Palette Exteriors	Freddy	Rod	1	2pm 7/8	9am 15/8
			Materials Landscaping	Ben	Sarah	1	2pm 6/8	9am 14/8

BID PROTOCOLS

Every time someone adheres to a protocol, a fairy gets his wings. These small acts of discipline contribute to a culture of respect for process, they also save you a monumental amount of time. Simple things like how you name files, manage version control, respond to bid emails, can make life easier and frees up time you don't have. Let people know what your bid protocols are at the outset, and don't accept any deviation.

Here are some of the bid protocols we use:

BID FILE STRUCTURE

A filing structure for all documents relating to the bid, to make sure everyone can easily find what they need on every bid

BID CONTROL SHEET

The primary bid management tool, ensures that everyone working on the bid knows the components of the bid, the elements needed for compliance, the timescales for delivery

BID EMAILS

An email organization guide, to make it easy to search and find what you need on emails in the final stages of a bid

VERSION CONTROL

Rules for managing revisions, to save time and avoid multiple copies of responses

TWO COLUMN TEMPLATES

A template used to plan out and structure content for a question response

CLARIFICATIONS LOG

This tool records the key clarifications for the bid and disseminates the information to the team

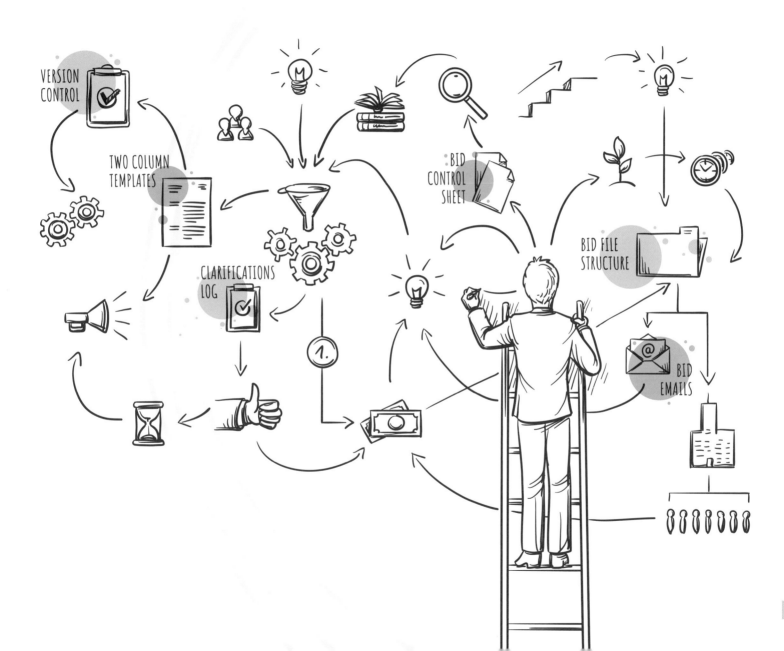

VERSION CONTROL

TWO COLUMN TEMPLATES

CLARIFICATIONS LOG

BID CONTROL SHEET

BID FILE STRUCTURE

BID EMAILS

BID KICK-OFF SESSION

Creating a winning bid requires corralling a large group of people to work together, to take on responsibilities usually in addition to their day jobs, working to strict deadlines, with the expectation that they will develop a kick-ass bid. This is why you need a kick-off session to help the group gel and focus on the big task that lies ahead of them.

Here is what the kick-off session is for:

+ Sharing your intelligence.
+ Agreeing bid protocols.
+ Building on the control sheet.
+ Allocating work for the bid period.
+ Agreeing the timelines.

Here are some tips for getting the most out of your kick-off session:

+ Locate the event away from the usual workplace, get people away from distractions.
+ Have a two-stage session. Stage one comes before the bid is out. People then have time to go away and get creative for stage two, which is when the bid is released.
+ Provide food, refreshments and regular comfort breaks.

Put your best people on the bid.

Use our control sheet for managing the bid - we haven't seen anything in bidding that the control sheet couldn't handle.

Set up bid protocols, simple things like how you name files, manage version control, and respond to bid emails, can make life easier and frees up time you don't have.

Hold a bid kick-off session to get your teammates gelling and focused on what lies ahead of them.

BUYER
ENGAGEMENT

At various points in this book, we talk about doing your buyer engagement before the bid becomes a bid. This period is your safe zone for asking the idiot questions and the clever ones too. Once you enter a procurement process, in the interests of fairness and transparency all questions directed to the buyer may be shared with all bidders. So, you lose the opportunity for open dialogue.

GOVERNMENT/PUBLIC SECTOR

Public sector buyers have very clear protocols around engagement, and the fastest way to get yourself kicked out of the competition is to breach those. If they say ask all questions through a portal, you ask all questions through a portal. You do not email individuals. On high value/high profile contracts some twitchy procurement officers will report you without hesitation, so just play the game and do exactly as you are told.

Remember:

+ Do not ask any questions that are going to reveal to the competition where your thinking is at. Some bidders engage in counter-intelligence by asking fake questions just to throw off their competitors.

+ Do not ask questions that will antagonize the buyer by asking them to reconfirm information that you should be able to work out for yourself.

+ If you have a valid question that the buyer repeatedly fails to answer properly, then accept they are fudging, trying to buy time, or just don't know.

These procurements will usually include market engagement events such as open-days, pre-bid conferences and bid openings open to all competitors. The format includes a presentation about the project from the buyer followed by a formal Q&A. If you are attending one of these events, you can gather great intel at registration, during coffee breaks, lunch, and at the end of the day.

Here are some essential tips for working a market engagement event:

+ Ask good questions, prepare some beforehand, keep them brief, don't ramble.

+ Introduce yourself to each of the buyer's team.

+ Observe the buyer's team personalities, power hierarchies and dynamics.

+ Discreetly map the competition.

+ Take pictures - but remember to get permission first.

And the biggest tip, see if you can get an independent professional researcher to attend in their own capacity. Without the burden of a name badge, they can ask obvious questions and soak up some good competitor intel.

DURING PROCUREMENT

In very complex bids, buyers will have a set timetable of meetings with each bidder covering different topics or workstreams. These are called by a variety of names, but often referred to as 'dialogue sessions', and are used to develop solutions that need input from bidders. When you are preparing for a dialogue session, it is really important that you are prepared. Dialogue sessions are often organized around topics, for example, on a hospital construction bid you would to expect to see a dedicated workstream for legal and commercial issues, construction, design and facilities management.

Before you attend a dialogue meeting find out the names and roles of each person from the buyer's side, so you can make sure you match them in expertise and seniority. When in a dialogue meeting, the most important thing is to listen. Confirm their requirements, ask enough questions to get a real feel on where their pain and drivers are coming from. Be careful that the questioning doesn't last too long because they can become frustrated if you are not feeding anything back to them.

I have been in two competitions now where I have seen the opposition kicked out for their unprofessional behavior at a competitive dialogue meeting. In both instances, the bidders were so stubborn and argumentative that the buyer decided right there and then that they did not want to work with the bidder. Behavior in these dialogue sessions is really important, it is where you start to build rapport and your working relationship.

A key purpose of the dialogue meeting involves kite-flying. This means you are flying some outlying ideas to test how far their thinking will go. Most bidders do not have the confidence to do this, but in the competitions where we have been the most effective, we have gone in with one kite-flyer, one observer and the senior person. The senior person is never the kite-flyer because they always have to keep their seniority. The kite-flyer has to be the most disposable person, because if it is too radical, that person should not be seen again. What you are doing is testing the waters as to how open the buyer is to pushing the boundaries, and you do that in a structured, smart, subtle way so they do not even know what they are experiencing. All the while, your observer is looking at how they are reacting to your concepts. People do not have to tell you – you can see it in their faces. You are looking to see where the lights shine.

HOW TO BEHAVE WITH YOUR BUYER

Just be human and likeable - enthusiasm, interest and passion will come across if it's genuine. Be sure to engage every single member of the buyer's team in discussion. Take notes of what was said and agreed. Observe their reactions to what is being said by your side. Afterwards, respond to clarifications raised at the meeting, fully and promptly.

DO'S

+ Respect
+ Openness and trust
+ Can-do, will-do attitudes
+ Commitment
+ Enthusiasm
+ Constructive challenge

DON'TS

+ Turn up without knowing exactly who you are meeting
+ Focus on the problems without providing a solution
+ Bore them with PowerPoint presentations
+ Be evasive if you are asked a question
+ Fail to follow through on actions you promised to do
+ Go in for the hard sell

PRIVATE SECTOR

Engagement with the private sector can be a lot more straightforward. However, a degree of caution is needed in private sector bidding. Our observation is that a lot of RFPs from the private sector are sloppy and not thought through. Buyers are not clear about what they want. This presents a big opportunity and a big risk.

If the buyer is dependent on you for their thinking and needs a lot of hand-holding, your engagement will focus heavily on unpacking all their issues and defining their pain points. But here's the burn. You can very easily find yourself in a position where you are presenting them with problems that are bigger than their pain, that they cannot influence or change.

One of the most effective engagement strategies that suits private sector buyers is to highlight where they are vulnerable to disruption. You show them how you have their back. "This is what I have been thinking about on your behalf" or "This is what your competitors are doing" or "This is what your sector is doing." Only do this, if (a) you understand the industry well, (b) you work with the buyer's competitors and (c) the buyer is a highly functioning person who gets it and wants a competitive edge.

Do your buyer engagement before the bid becomes a bid – you can ask all the idiot questions and the clever ones too.

Respect that government/ public sector buyers have very strict protocols for engagements, the fastest way to get yourself kicked out of the competition is to breach those.

When engaging with the buyer just be human and likeable - enthusiasm, interest and passion will come across if it's genuine.

Be careful your engagement doesn't present the buyer with problems that are bigger than their pain, that they cannot influence or change.

WRITING
AND REVIEW

At the end of the day, your written responses to the questions will either win you or lose you the bid. When you put a really strong bid response next to a really weak one, the difference is stark and the buyer's heart rate starts to reduce, their comfort levels increase. They are looking for a safe option to award their contract to. The only way they can judge that is on what you put in front of them. What you put in front of them matters.

I have heard so many people say RFPs do not win bids, they are just part of the process. Maybe that is correct in some places. In other places, I can certainly guarantee you that RFPs can lose you a bid. If they can lose you a bid, they have got to be a major part of winning a bid and in winning a bid, what you write in these questions is key to everything.

ENROLL ON OUR WRITING AND REVIEW ELEARNING COURSE TO SHARPEN YOUR BID WRITING SKILLS
shinebidservices.com/elearning

MANAGING THE WRITING PROCESS

Managing the planning, writing, review and editing process smoothly is key to developing refined written responses and hit deadlines. Robust management of the writing process is necessary, especially on complex bids where you could have up to 10 lead authors and as many contributors in play. Having sat across from authors, clients and colleagues, I've seen significant confusion amongst them over what they were meant to be writing and by when. Use the control sheet to clearly name the lead author who will own the response, and the different contributors who will feed into it.

Deciding who writes what is a really important thing to get right. Question whether the authors are the right person for the job. It sounds silly but can they write well? Do they know enough about the subject? Will they have enough time? Just make sure to leave enough time to rescue the responses if you need to. The control sheet is your trusted friend in this.

PLAN, ANSWER PLANNING OR STORYBOARDING

People tend to rush into writing without thinking about what they are going to write or why. This is how to lose bids. Developing your bid strategy first, then moving on to answer planning reduces rework and improves the quality of responses. We always make time to discuss the question, plan out our responses and capture this plan in a brief 'Answer Plan' or 'Storyboard'. This provides the author with an agreed structure and content plan to ensure we score high and appeal to the evaluator. The planning process gathers expert input for the author, helps crystallize the win strategy and highlights gaps in the offer.

We host answer planning workshops to help writers. These are facilitated workshops held early on with the author, facilitator, bid boss and other expert contributors. We also draw up answer plans / storyboards. This is a one pager of instructions and information to help the author. The storyboards use the '2-column' format, with headings on the left and content prompts on the right to structure the response. They also contain suggested word counts next to each heading to help the author balance how much to write for each section.

Using the answer plans, either write responses from scratch, extract expert knowledge and write it up or manage and support others to write responses. You can also hire a bid writer. A professional skilled in writing bid documentation could save you a lot of time.

ANSWER PLAN TEMPLATE

Part 1 - Author Instructions

Question ref	[Question XX]
Version	[1.0, etc]
Question	[Insert from tender documentation]
Weighting	[XX%] of quality submission
Page limit	[X] sides of A4
Word count	[Either as instructed in tender or use 500 words per page as guide]
Lead author	[Name]
Contributors	[Name], [Name]
Getting top marks	[Insert scoring criteria]

Win Themes to reflect in this response	[These will come from your win strategy workshop and write up] [List the win themes that are relevant to the question]
How to use this template	Keep all responses in the two-column format, it helps with the reviews of the responses, checking the balance of content and ensuring the responses go in to the design layout process smoothly. **What are the Yellow highlights?** Use yellow to highlight any prompts for authors – e.g. notes on what should be written or suggestions for content or where to source information. **What are the Magenta highlights?** These are prompts to the designers to direct how you want the response to appear in design, for example, highlight where you want something to stand out or text for turning into an infographic.

Part 2 - Answer Plan Template

PARAGRAPH HEADINGS	NOTES FOR CONTENT
Intro	Key message 1 Key message 2 Key message 3
Heading 1 [XX words]	**Subheading 1** Point to address 1 Point to address 2
Heading 2 [XX words]	**Subheading 1** Point to address 1 Point to address 2
Heading 3 [XX words]	**Subheading 1** Point to address 1 Point to address 2
Heading 4 [XX words]	**Subheading 1** Point to address 1 Point to address 2
Heading 5 [XX words]	Continue as required....

DO YOU UNDERSTAND THE QUESTION?

Remember the advice of teachers before an exam? Read the question properly!
Break down the question to help you interpret what is being asked for.

Example:

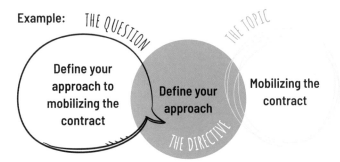

Look for the directive or the action words. Here it is "define your approach". You do not talk about just mobilization. Your approach to mobilization is to talk about "how" you do things rather than what you do. Now that you have addressed the directive it's time to look at the topic. Mobilization - describe the activity. You then look at your win theme matrix – accelerated delivery is one of your win themes so you need to state you do it in 90 days or 10 minutes or in 60 seconds flat or whatever it is.

Example:

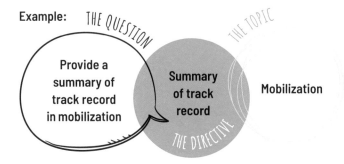

For this question you write a completely different answer, they want to know what you have actually done, so you provide an excessive amount of case studies so that you give them the level of certainty you can deliver.

HOW TO WRITE A GOOD RESPONSE

Answer the f@%&ing question (IN FULL!) – you would be amazed how many people fail at this first hurdle ... whether the author has spent too much time on one aspect of the question or whether the author just doesn't understand the question in full. I have sat down side-by-side with so many writers and can tell you some read the first three words and start writing. They completely miss the bit after the comma on the last line, and they have just lost 15 points. You might get away with this in private sector bidding, the buyer might come back to you with hints to help you out. In the public sector, the buyer won't give you a second chance. They will move on to your competitor, who has done two sides of A4 with a flow chart and a named person responsible and shown application in their track record. Suddenly the buyer has certainty and it allows them to give you a really low score. It is not that they do not like you, it is that you are already coming across as sloppy and untrustworthy, and the other bidder is coming across as thorough and solid.

DON'T REPEAT

Don't fall into the trap of just repeating the buyer's requirements – this is something we often see when a company does not have a strong offer. It is not enough to just say that your team will work collaboratively, and you will meet regularly with the buyer etc., etc. You need to show HOW you will do what they want. It is like me selling you a diet pill by stating that it will make you lose weight and when you ask how, I just keep repeating it will make you lose weight by taking it ...

KNOW THE STORY, OR FIND SOMEONE WHO DOES

If you, as a writer, do not know the story – for example you do not know what your mobilization plan would be – sit with your subject matter expert and ask them to talk you through it. You might need to consult multiple subject matter experts in this way for one response – especially if it's a very technical or nuanced topic – for example how does mobilization interface with security systems – here you'll need the security person to input. You can get a really complex question about an area that you know very little about resolved in half a day if you have discipline and access to a subject matter expert.

THE 'SO WHAT?' CHECK

This is a really powerful question. What is the significance of your answer? What benefit does this provide the buyer? Authors will sometimes waffle or not get to the point. This is inefficient and will make the evaluator switch off. Always ask yourself "What is the significance of what I am writing?"

PROVE IT!

Evidence takes the promises and aspirations and makes them real. Evidence gives confidence to the evaluators and makes you a credible potential partner.

WRITING IN IMAGES

Go through your response and ask "Where could I graphically make my points more strongly and would it be better to have an organization chart here, have a flow diagram, or infographic?" Make sure that all graphics are referenced or have a particular purpose or message, because images used incorrectly can throw an evaluator off. Carefully review all graphics in context to ensure they are sending the right messages.

Graphics do's and don'ts:

+ Never throw in random graphics to fill space or if they are meaningless

+ Using images cleverly won't affect the word count – such as by sneaking in captions with a disclaimer 'This page is not word counted'

+ Ensure they are accompanied by captions that add value

As branding is going on at the same time, there are key links to be made. Some elements of your written message may tie in to the visual brand and the overall strapline (such as a branded impact box in every section or an icon used throughout the bid to emphasize a certain message). Keep in mind how the two will need to be tied/developed together.

EXAMPLE IMAGE CAPTIONS

Poor caption: Outside Space

Good caption: A vibrant outdoor space designed to complement the essence of the historical architecture

Excellent caption: Mixing the old and new - a public realm that pays homage to your history, allows people to interact and has plenty of open space ready for community activation. Here you can engage local people and create a real sense of place from day one.

REVIEW PROCESS

Review responses to assess if they are well-structured, clear, have the right tone, reflect the win strategy, answer the question and have an appealing offer to the buyer. Use the control sheet to schedule in the reviews. Reviews can be done in joint review sessions with the bid boss, or remotely as track-changes or note mark-ups of word documents. If you have formal joint in-person reviews, referred to as '50% Draft Review' or '80% Draft Review', get the right people at review sessions. It's no use having 10 reviewers but no decision-makers at answer review sessions. It is important that in advance you give people time and ask them to read the responses so they come prepared with comments and don't waste your time in the meeting by reading. Get the bid boss or authorized representative at the planning, review and sign-off sessions so you can have the necessary discussion about the final content.

THE GOAL OF ALL REVIEWS IS TO:

+ Make things better than when you started
+ Find and plug gaps
+ Incorporate wider views for richer answers
+ Check we have used our strategy and tools to get to the right stage
+ Ready ourselves for the next stage
+ Put recovery actions in place

Take the time to plan your answer before writing. Use our answer planning template or storyboard to help with this.

Make sure you answer the f@%&ing question, read and then re-read the question to make sure you don't miss anything.

If you don't know the story behind what you're writing in your response, then find someone who does.

Focus your response on how you will deliver the buyer's requirements to avoid falling into the trap of just repeating their requirements.

Provide evidence to back-up your claims.

Go through your responses and identify where a graphic could make the point more strongly.

Schedule in reviews of the responses.

PRODUCTION

You will need to decide at the outset how much money, time and effort you are going to spend on the production side of the bid. Here at ShineBid, we design our bids to look like magazines so they are highly readable, portable and exciting to look at. For dense bids, we split them down, still magazine size, with nothing over 100 to 110 pages.

Our production process is fairly efficient, we build everything in Word, and have a concept design developed, usually in InDesign or Illustrator. Once we have a concept, we artwork the whole document into an artwork design package. We find this delivers a good quality end product and enhances the impact of the written content, aiding navigation for evaluators and drawing out key elements of the offer.

If you have the luxury of an in-house creative designer or know a freelance designer to work on your bid you can create a really strong brief. This should all be coming from your strategy input. Once you have your concept, and you have worked out how your concepts define your bid brand, you are going to apply this liberally or scantily all over your bid, depending on what point you are trying to make. If you are going to design your bid, you design it as per your control sheet. In a major bid with us, that control sheet would have about 11 versions, so it is your master plan for how you are going to deal with the bid.

VERSION CONTROL

Most bid blunders and time delays can be attributed to poor version control. Sometimes you can have 20 people inputting to a bid, a lot of them on different sections, misnaming files, using different collaborative software. Even though you might have a smart platform solution, you will get the non-compliant person who will mess it up. We use the control sheets to track the status of responses and communicate the protocol for version control at the start of the bid. We have a filing convention for names allowing only one version of the document to exist on your system.

DIGITAL SUBMISSIONS

An increasing number of RFPs are submitted digitally. For character uploads cut and paste into the portal from the original text. Don't write original copy into the portal directly. Check character limits on uploads against instructions in the requirements. We had a situation on a very important legal bid where the buyer's written instructions required 4,000 words, but the portal was set to accept only 4,000 characters, the buyer made a mistake between words and characters. We were ready to load 4,000 words, however, our upload stopped at 4,000 characters. We had enough time to edit and rewrite to get it compliant. Imagine the panic if we did not have the time. Of course, you can go back and complain but it is too late.

Make sure you leave plenty of time before and after uploading. The worst upload we have ever done was with 37 seconds to spare, which I would never recommend, but typically we will aim to upload with at least three hours to go. There have been plenty of nightmare scenarios, especially when you are working in different time zones and there is a big traffic migration to that site in a different country. We think it is 02:00am in the morning and uploading gigabytes of material, but actually it is 5:00 p.m. in somebody else's world. You are working with a global company that has 10,000 bids going up, the site just cannot take it and you need every minute of those three hours to get all your material up. Plan, calendar and stick to your schedule. Carry out a system test run a day or two before the deadline to make sure you are familiar with it. And then allow enough time to upload your submission on the day.

LOGISTICS

This may sound really trivial, but make sure you have an ironclad delivery option in place. Your production does not end until you have the bid in its delivery box with its brown wrapping paper and its no-logo address with a registered logistics company delivering it before the deadline and getting a signed receipt, then the bid is in – not until then. If you're delivering the bid via a courier, or a team member delivering the bid in person or a taxi waiting for you outside, make sure you have a back-up if it falls through. Then get a delivery receipt from the place you delivered it to.

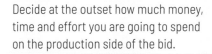

Decide at the outset how much money, time and effort you are going to spend on the production side of the bid.

For digital submissions, make sure you do a test run, and leave plenty of time before and after uploading.

Your production does not end until you have the bid in its delivery box, make sure you have an ironclad delivery option in place.

EXECUTIVE SUMMARY

The entire purpose of your bid's executive summary is to hero your win strategy. Clearly articulate how your solutions and the unique benefits they bring address their buyer issues. It is your shop window, where your big sell helps you stand out amongst your competitors. It is arguably the most valuable component of a bid. Even if it's not a requirement, my advice is to write one and submit it. The buyer can disregard it in the evaluation – but that doesn't mean it won't catch the eye of a big wig or find its way into the workbag of a decision-maker to read on their commute home.

HOW TO STRUCTURE THE EXECUTIVE SUMMARY

How you structure the executive summary is driven by who you think you need to influence. If you are trying to influence a CEO and she is the biggest decision-maker, pitch it predominantly to her. If you think the biggest decision-maker is going to be a practical operational person, again, pitch it to him, but remember you will have a wider audience reading the document too.

The executive summary is also the time where you have to commit yourself. Do not put out executive summaries with weasel words - language such as "we will endeavor to" or "we will ensure" or "we will develop." Just commit, make strong and clear statements "by March of this year, we will have delivered X, Y and Z" or "our mobilization will get you established within 16 days". If you think by being ambiguous you leave the possibility to backtrack from commitments, usually because they are un-costed, then accept that you have increased your chances of losing.

Not all bids warrant a substantial crafted piece of writing. In the past, we have used a postcard as an executive summary, to say "Why us?" on one side and on the other side "Because we will deliver you X, Y and Z." On another bid, a bookmark doubled as our executive summary. We needed to create a bookmark because the bid submission was made up of five volumes. We also knew that the buyer wasn't keen on excessive flashiness, a glossy magazine style executive summary would not have done us any favors. To this day, the buyer has kept the bookmark on his desk, to keep reminding our client of what they promised in their bid.

POPULATOR TOOL

Executive Summary Populator Tool

FEATURE	COMMITMENT	BENEFIT	STATS
Headline message/ solution/ feature/ offer/ differentiator/ win theme	What commitments can you make to make it real?	What's the benefit/ impact for the buyer?	Do you have any statistics/ numbers to back it up?

WHEN TO WRITE IT

Write the executive summary after you have your win strategy, after you have developed the solutions to the buyer issues and drafted the bulk of the proposal content. To help you draft the document use the 'Populator' tool, which is about capturing every big commitment, discriminator, and benefit as you go along, during the bid process, so at the right time you have the components that make up your executive summary.

TIPS FOR DEVELOPING A POWERFUL EXECUTIVE SUMMARY

1 Have one author write the document.

2 Don't slip in something that's not covered in the bid.

3 Write original copy. Don't rehash sections of the bid.

4 Commit!

5 Don't cram in everything you can think of.

6 Make sure it stands out from the rest of the bid, keep the bid brand, but use a different color.

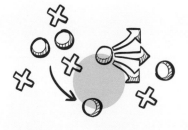

The executive summary may be your last opportunity to get your message across. It can be a game-changer in a close competition.

Even if it's not a requirement write one and submit it. Let the buyer decide if they want to read it.

It doesn't have to be an obvious document. Take a subtle approach; put your big sell on a post card or a bookmark.

Write it after you have crafted your win strategy, after solution development, and after the bulk of the proposal content has been drafted.

INTERVIEWS AND PRESENTATIONS

The bid interview or presentation comes soon after the bid submission. It is your last opportunity to impress the buyer. This is when you need to ramp up, not wind down. You can rest after it's done. Most of the problems we see result from leaving the presentation preparation to the last minute. Be like our framework client, the presentation was two days after the bid deadline. We started working on their presentation with them mid-way through the bid period. On the day of the interview the team were fully prepped, relaxed and ready to perform.

Before you start working on your presentation you need to nail down the following:

+ Who is your audience? Who is on the panel?

+ What do they want to hear? What's important to them?

+ What are their instructions or guidelines for the presentation?

+ What's the venue and the room layout of the place where the presentation is to be held?

STRUCTURING YOUR PRESENTATION

HOW NOT TO DO IT

The following structure for a presentation is a sure-fire route to losing a bid, especially a close bid. Don't feel bad if you're guilty of having used it.

+ Who we are
+ Our journey
+ Our team

+ Our services
+ Our generic solutions
+ Any questions

Here's why. It's all about you. The client has a clear and distinct need and listening to you is not one of them. You are there to make their life easier and by using this approach you are asking too much. They should not have to interpret how you can help them.

HERE'S HOW TO DO IT

Simply flip your approach – look at things from the perspective of the buyer, be totally focused on them.

+ You (the buyer)
+ Your challenge/ need/ problem
+ Our solution to your challenge/ need/ problem
+ Our track record in delivering similar challenges/ needs/ problems (evidence)
+ How our solution is better than our competitors
+ Any questions

You are spelling out your solution in relation to their needs.

DEFINING YOUR MESSAGES

HOW NOT TO DO IT

You have some guidance from the buyer on the areas they want you to cover in your presentation, you dive straight in.

+ You allocate 10mins to Shahzad on technical, 10min to Emilie on commercial, 10min for Peter to top and tail.

+ They develop their slides independently in their respective specialist areas.

+ You amalgamate the slides into a 100-slide deck packed with text, diagrams and data.

+ You describe in detail all the features of your products/services without relating the benefits to the client.

You will end up with a hodgepodge of ideas that are confusing and don't flow together. You will lose the audience's interest, and the bid.

HERE'S HOW TO DO IT

Be clear about what you want the audience to take away and use storytelling to take them on a journey, delivering key messages, while keeping them engaged.

+ Define exactly what you want to achieve in the presentation – Do you want to impress them? Reassure them?

+ Once you know your objective, draw out all the key parts of your bid that reinforces this.

+ Then distil this into three or four key points – studies show people can remember only three or four things in a presentation.

+ Then put this into a logical flow.

TELL A CRISP, CLEAN STORY

Jerry Weissman, *corporate presentations coach*

DELIVERING WITH CONFIDENCE

HOW NOT TO DO IT

+ Skimp on hiring a presentation skills coach.

+ Have people read from notes, avoid eye contact, fidget, and pace.

+ Don't bother with rehearsals – the presenters know what they're doing.

+ Don't do a time check – overrun is no big deal.

HERE'S HOW TO DO IT

Don't pretend to be someone else. Just be a better version of yourself. By this, we mean playing up strengths and playing down weaknesses.

+ Get a presentation skills coach in – everyone will benefit however experienced they are.

+ Film the presenters' rehearsals, play it back to them, they might find it cringeworthy, but it's a good way to give feedback.

+ Presenters should adopt confident body language – see box below.

+ They should be authentic and present in a comfortable conversational tone.

+ Your team needs to show some enthusiasm and energy.

+ Do a run through with timings to avoid overruns.

+ Rehearse. Rehearse. Rehearse – it will help your team refine its message further.

+ Make sure you produce a 'leave behind document'.

THE CLINTON BOX

Based on a Bill Clinton anecdote, if you don't know what to do with your hands, imagine a box in front of your chest and belly and contain your hand movements within. Indicates trustworthiness

HOLDING THE BALL

As if you're holding a basketball between your hands. Indicates confidence and in control

PYRAMID HANDS

Clasp your hands together in a pyramid shape. Indicates self-assurance and feeling relaxed

WIDE STANCE

Strong and steady with feet about a shoulder width apart. Indicates confidence and in control

PALMS UP

Have your hands hip height and arms wide open, palms facing up. Indicates openness and honesty

Source: Centre for Body Language

HANDLING TOUGH QUESTIONS

One thing you can be certain of is that there will be some tough questions in the Q&A session after the presentation.

HOW NOT TO DO IT

+ Do ten minutes of preparation for the Q&A session just before you head in.

+ Have your most senior person jump in to answer every question.

+ Start "piling on" – this is when everyone in your team chips into the answer just because.

+ Be defensive when asked about a sensitive topic.

+ Be evasive because you don't want to commit.

+ Make stuff up because you don't know the answer, or you didn't read the bid.

HERE'S HOW TO DO IT

+ Know your bid inside out.

+ Agree beforehand on who will cover which topics.

+ Agree who is responsible for answering what types of questions.

+ Spend as much time prepping for the Q&A as you do for the presentation.

+ Prepare for tough questions:

  − Look at the weaknesses of your offer

  − Look at the strength of the opposition

  − Write down the toughest questions you can possibly think of and prep for them repeatedly

  − Then move onto the typical standard ones and prep for them

+ Always do closing remarks, don't end your presentation on a Q&A.

+ Make sure you produce a 'leave behind document'.

DEVELOPING YOUR PRESENTATION IN THREE STEPS

You can get your interview or presentation planned, rehearsed and polished in three steps. Do it over non-consecutive days because you'll need the time in between to do the work.

STORY DEVELOPMENT

+ Define what you want to achieve
+ Brainstorm ideas
+ Pick the 4 – 5 key messages
+ Order the messages into a logical flow
+ Decide who the presenters will be
+ Agree other media assets e.g. material, handouts, models

SLIDE DESIGN & REFINEMENT

+ Finalize the structure and content for the presentation
+ Prepare for tough questions
+ Produce your 'leave behind document'

DELIVERY SKILLS & REHEARSAL

+ Buy in presentation skills coaching
+ Practice and rehearse the presentation at least twice with timings
+ Practice answering expected questions effectively

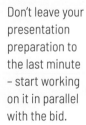

Don't leave your presentation preparation to the last minute – start working on it in parallel with the bid.

Structure your presentation around the perspective of the buyer - their challenge/ need/ problem – then spell out your solution in relation to their needs.

Be absolutely clear on what you want to achieve in the presentation.

Tell a crisp, clean story – focus on 4-5 key messages.

Bring in a presentation skills coach to hone your delivery styles.

Practice answering the tough questions you could get during the Q&A.

Rehearse. Rehearse. Rehearse.

REVIEW,
FEEDBACK

THE PROBLEMS WITH REVIEWS

Proper post-bid reviews are rarely done even though they are one of the most important drivers in increasing your win rate. Whether you win or lose, you need to understand the reasons behind why.

Most organizations we work with do some post-bid analysis, typically in a group session format. But they find these sessions to be completely ineffective. Their people don't like to be subject to scrutiny and will try their best to get out of the session. The sessions are usually unstructured, and if handled badly, descend into a free-for-all blame session. If it's a lost bid, the loss is usually attributed to price – broad feedback like this will tend to close down further lines of investigation into the real reasons behind a loss. If it's a win, there will be backslapping all around. After the session, comes the write-up, which is invariably toned down, in the published version, to smooth out any contentious issues. It is then filed away, never to be seen again. If your learning doesn't lead to action, it's a pointless exercise. The net result is repeating the same mistakes and no improvement in your win rate.

These are some of the problems with post-bid reviews, and our solutions for addressing them.

PROBLEM:

Getting people to
open up without fear
of recriminations

SOLUTION:

+ Get an independent facilitator to host the review session.
+ Set out what you want to achieve and share this with the participants beforehand so they know what to expect.
+ Get the participants to generate their own ground rules for behavior at the session.
+ Focus the agenda on what was learnt about the buyer, your process and team working, instead of dwelling on what went wrong or well.
+ Send participants an online survey, make it anonymous to capture as many views as possible.

PROBLEM:

Pinpointing the underlying win/lose factors that made the difference

SOLUTION:

+ Get feedback from the buyer – hear directly from them on your dealmakers and dealbreakers.

+ Filter through the review session feedback with a core group to prioritize the main issues.

+ Do a root cause analysis on the prioritized feedback to identify the underlying factors.

PROBLEM:

Sharing and acting on
the learning

SOLUTION:

+ An agenda focused on what was learnt will result in a write
  up that doesn't need to be toned down.

+ Do a 'So What?' analysis on what you've learnt to generate
  actions to implement next time.

+ Build your learning into your bid process, for example, you
  might decide to develop checklists to use on the next bid.

+ Let your biggest successes and failures become epic stories
  that your people can tell over and over again. You want them
  to become company folklore, that are told by bid bosses to
  bid teams and new employees for many years to come.

AN EFFECTIVE POST-BID REVIEW PROCESS

SELF-ASSESSMENT

Hold a group session with the bid team and/or send out a questionnaire

Do it as soon as the bid is submitted, while its fresh in everyone's minds

The session must be controlled, structured, and moderated by an independent facilitator

The four questions you need to ask your team:

1 What did you learn about the buyer?

2 What did you learn about how well you worked together?

3 What were the impacts for the organization?

4 How did you grow your skills?

BUYER FEEDBACK

Insist on an in-person briefing from the buyer. You need to hear what made the difference.

This is offered as standard in the public sector, but it's much harder to get feedback from the private sector buyer. You can ask them to agree to post bid feedback before you bid – you could send them an online survey.

The four questions you need to ask your buyer:

1 Why didn't we win?

2 Did we understand/interpret your business requirements?

3 Did we make any mistakes?

4 What could we do differently in future?

SHARING AND ACTING ON LEARNING

Carry out a 'So What?' analysis on your learning for example consider what this mean for your processes - do you need to develop new ones, get rid of redundant ones, or modify existing ones.

The two main questions you need to address:

1 What do we absolutely need to do?

2 What can we do about it now?

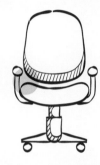

Reflect on your losses and your wins.

Hold a bid review session as soon as the bid is submitted, while it's fresh in everyone's mind.

Don't just sit on the learning – share it, and act on it. This is where the real pay-off lies.

Make sure you get an in-person briefing from the buyer.

IN **CONCLUSION**

Bidding is a tough business but is seriously rewarding when things come together, and you land that big win. The ShineBid Winning Masterplan™ is your trusted guide through the process – keep it close by.

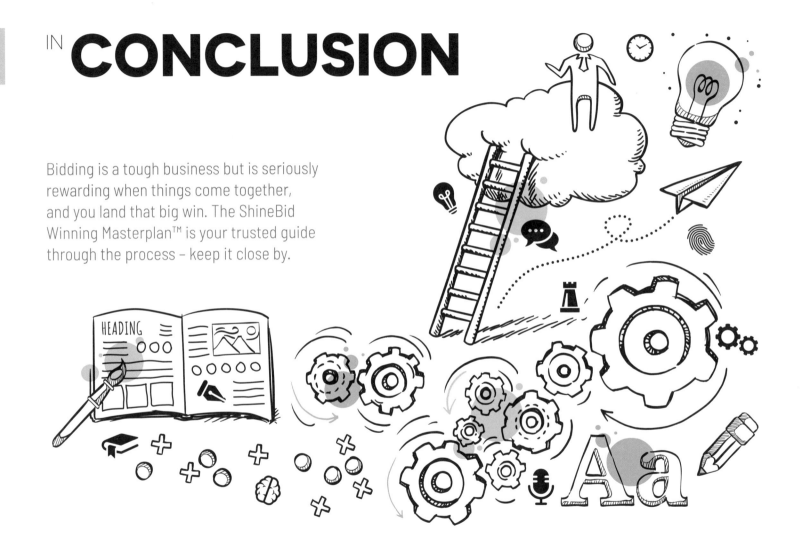

GOOD
LUCK.
ENJOY
THE RIDE.

RESOURCES

DOWNLOAD OUR FREE EBOOKS

Download the following ebooks from
shinebidservices.com/resources

+ How to Bid for Government Contracts in the USA
+ How to Bid for Government Contracts in the UK

DOWNLOAD OUR FREE GUIDES AND TEMPLATES

Download the following guides and templates from
shinebidservices.com/resources

+ The ShineBid Winning Masterplan™
+ Win Theme Matrix
+ Control Sheet Template
+ Answer Plan Template
+ Populator Tool

ENROL ON ELEARNING

Enrol on our ShineBid elearning courses at
shinebidservices.com/elearning

IN THIS SECTION

You can also find the following resources overleaf

+ Buyer Intel - The Key Questions
+ Competitor Intel - The Key Questions
+ Win Theme Matrix
+ The ShineBid Winning Masterplan™
+ Control Sheet Template
+ Answer Plan Template
+ Populator Tool

**BUYER INTEL
THE KEY QUESTIONS**

WIN THEME MATRIX

		Question					
		1 **Team**	**2** **Planning**	**3** **Programme**	**4** **Logistics**	**5** **Supply Chain**	**6** **Etc**
Big Sell and Win Themes	Leader in innovation	✓	✓	✓	✓	✓	✓
	Best in class collaborative working	✓	✓	✓		✓	
	National player with a local team	✓	✓			✓	
	Apprenticeship scheme for local young people	✓			✓	✓	
	Etc.						
	Evaluation weighting %						

Initial documents issued

GO TO MARKET

PRE ISSUE

FIT TO FIGHT

DEFINE STRATEGY

Driving the sale »

Driving the win »

STAGE ONE

TARGET	CUSTOMER SEGMENTATION	CREATE THE GAP	PROJECT INTELLIGENCE	WIN STRATEGY	SOLUTION DEVELOPMENT
Define what you're pursuing	Define your customer segments	Stand out from the competition	Early engagement	Strategy kick-off session	Invent
Define your blockers to growth	Review segments	Define your value proposition	Gathering information	Define the big sell	Adapt
Find the solution	Develop segment strategies	Take a stand	Turning information into intelligence	Agree bid protocols	Develop workstreams
Get tactical		Build value through your brand	Share the intelligence	Agree proposal messaging	

STAGE TWO

Take action	Identify the support you need	Generate compelling campaigns	Update and share intelligence	Define the big sell	Generate solutions

LIVE PROPOSAL

IMPLEMENT STRATEGY

SELL STRATEGY

BRANDING	SET-UP & MANAGEMENT	FORMAL CLIENT ENGAGEMENT	WRITING & REVIEW	PRODUCTION	EXECUTIVE SUMMARY	INTERVIEWS & PRESENTATION
Develop a concept	Build the team	Dialogue preparation	The questions	Design management	Position summary	Plan
Define the media assets	Develop a concept	During dialogue	Planning your response	Submission	Define platform/medium	Prepare
	Create proposal protocol	After dialogue	Editing	Compliance and quality control	Write	Deliver
			CV's		Design and produce	
			Case studies			
			Making your writing compelling			
			Reviewing your responses			

Refine your brand	Review your set-up assumptions	Analyse your client	Generate better responses	Blow them away with your proposal	Executive Summary get it right	Meeting them for the last time as bidders

CONTROL SHEET TEMPLATE

Headlines

PROJECT	[Enter project name here]
BID BOSS	[Name][Email][Phone][Mobile]
KEY BID CONTACTS	
KEY DEADLINES	[Key Deadline][Date]

Key Dates and Bid Production Timetable

ACTIVITY	DEADLINE
Agree bid strategy and bid production actions	[Date]
Answer planning for questions and templates completed	[Date]
Develop bid brand	[Date]
Issue question response templates	[Date]
Drafts produced by authors/contributors	[Date]
Sign off on bid brand	[Date]
Authors issue first drafts of responses and appendices	[Date]
Review of drafts	[Date]
Update of response drafts and appendices	[Date]
Clarifications deadline	[Date]
Sign off of designed bid	[Date]
Print deadline	[Date]
Upload of submission	[Date]

Notes and submission requirements: [Insert any notes about the submission eg. Font size, file formats, page/word limits]

Detailed Control Sheet Content for Questions

[SECTION NAME]								
Ref	Question	Weighting (If applicable)	Response Headlines	Responsible	Contributors	Page Limits (or word count)	Draft Deadline	Final Deadline
[XX]	A schedule and details of the proposed materials, finishes and components to new and retained areas	15%	Materials Outline	Rod	Jane	1	2pm 6/8	9am 14/8
			Materials Palette Interiors	Jane	Rod	1	2pm 7/8	9am 15/8
			Materials Palette Exteriors	Freddy	Rod	1	2pm 7/8	9am 15/8
			Materials Landscaping	Ben	Sarah	1	2pm 6/8	9am 14/8

ANSWER PLAN TEMPLATE

Part 1 - Author Instructions

Question ref	[Question XX]
Version	[1.0, etc]
Question	[Insert from tender documentation]
Weighting	[XX%] of quality submission
Page limit	[X] sides of A4
Word count	[Either as instructed in tender or use 500 words per page as guide]
Lead author	[Name]
Contributors	[Name], [Name]
Getting top marks	[Insert scoring criteria]

Win Themes to reflect in this response	[These will come from your win strategy workshop and write up] [List the win themes that are relevant to the question]
How to use this template	Keep all responses in the two-column format, it helps with the reviews of the responses, checking the balance of content and ensuring the responses go in to the design layout process smoothly. **What are the Yellow highlights?** Use yellow to highlight any prompts for authors - e.g. notes on what should be written or suggestions for content or where to source information. **What are the Magenta highlights?** These are prompts to the designers to direct how you want the response to appear in design, for example, highlight where you want something to stand out or text for turning into an infographic.

Part 2 - Answer Plan Template

PARAGRAPH HEADINGS	NOTES FOR CONTENT
Intro	Key message 1 Key message 2 Key message 3
Heading 1 [XX words]	Subheading 1 Point to address 1 Point to address 2
Heading 2 [XX words]	Subheading 1 Point to address 1 Point to address 2
Heading 3 [XX words]	Subheading 1 Point to address 1 Point to address 2
Heading 4 [XX words]	Subheading 1 Point to address 1 Point to address 2
Heading 5 [XX words]	Continue as required....

POPULATOR TOOL

Executive Summary Populator Tool

FEATURE Headline message/ solution/ feature/ offer/ differentiator/ win theme	COMMITMENT What commitments can you make to make it real?	BENEFIT What's the benefit/ impact for the buyer?	STATS Do you have any statistics/ numbers to back it up?